PEER COACHING IN HIGHER EDUCATION

Barbara L. Gottesman

Rowman & Littlefield Education
A Division of
Rowman & Littlefield Publishers, Inc.
Lanham • New York • Toronto • Plymouth, UK

Published by Rowman & Littlefield Education
A division of Rowman & Littlefield Publishers, Inc.
A wholly owned subsidary of
The Rowman & Littlefield Publishing Group, Inc.
4501 Forbes Boulevard, Suite 200, Lanham, Maryland 20706
www.rowmaneducation.com

Estover Road, Plymouth PL6 7PY, United Kingdom

British Library Cataloguing in Publication Information Available

Library of Congress Cataloging-in-Publication Data
Gottesman, Barbara Little.
 Peer coaching in higher education / Barbara L. Gottesman.
   p. cm.
 ISBN 978-1-60709-413-5 (cloth : alk. paper) — ISBN 978-1-60709-414-2
(pbk. : alk. paper) — ISBN 978-1-60709-415-9 (electronic)
 1. College teachers—In-service training—United States—Case studies. 2.
College teaching—United States—Evaluation—Case studies. 3. Mentoring in
education—United States—Case studies. 4. Group work in education—United
States—Case studies. I. Title.
 LB1738.G66 2009
 378.1'25—dc22   2009020729

⊗™ The paper used in this publication meets the minimum requirements of
American National Standard for Information Sciences—Permanence of Paper
for Printed Library Materials, ANSI/NISO Z39.48-1992.
Printed in the United States of America

CONTENTS

INTRODUCTION

In 1994, the first edition of *Peer Coaching for Educators* was published. It was simply a handbook of how to implement this non-evaluative, non-judgmental process at the K–12 level. With 331 schools in our Effective Schools Training Program, we had many opportunities to test its application from theory to practice with a diverse group of teachers.

In 2000, the second edition refined the theory into practice of the process over several more states and many other adoptions. The practice of implementing peer coaching among the 150 partner schools in the South Carolina Center for the Advancement of Teaching and School Leadership was included. In 1990, Barbara Gottesman became the state site coordinator for a collaborative of five colleges and 42 professional development schools where peer coaching was also implemented. This state collaborative was among the first eight state sites selected as a partner in John Goodlad's National Network for Educational Renewal. With her colleagues from 25 sites and 16 states, she advocated peer coaching for leadership teams within the network.

As department chair for education at Columbia College in South Carolina and later as department chair for Educational Leadership at San José State University in California, Gottesman incorporated peer coaching in professional development school partnerships and in leadership graduate programs.

The peer coaching processes discussed in this book are the results of Gottesman's own experience in numerous schools, with two national networks, and in five universities. The process is thoroughly outlined with examples from various situations. Actual peer coaching exchanges are offered in an appendix so that professors and instructors will have examples of extended practices of peer coaching.

1

DEVOLUTION OF PEER COACHING

[T]he quality of adult relationships within a school has more to do with the quality and character of the school and with the accomplishments of students than any other factor.

(Barth, 1990, 163)

Never doubt that a small group of thoughtful committed people can change the world: indeed it's the only thing that ever has.

—Margaret Mead

CONCEPTUAL FRAMEWORK

In the magic triad of research, teaching, and service, research has always been the dominant factor for promotion and tenure. Traditionally, steps in the tenure and promotion process are in place to reward junior faculty with sufficient publications or a well-funded research agenda. In the 21st century, however, excellence in teaching is gaining in importance.

The idea that teaching in universities can be improved is gaining widespread acceptance among professors and instructors. The tradition that teachers in higher education provide instruction in their disciplines without being concerned about teaching techniques is rapidly becoming passé. The argument that professors cannot teach effectively because they have taken no education methods courses is specious. University professors and instructors today are seeking other ways to improve teaching in order to increase student learning.

In the promotion and tenure process, an evaluative observation by the department chair or the retention, tenure, and promotion committee often is the sole direct supervisory experience. Peer coaching is not a replacement for an evaluative observation by a department chair or committee. It is a process by which university professors and instructors can improve their teaching techniques by observing, giving feedback, and coaching each other.

Peer coaching consists of a model and a set of rules whereby two professors or instructors, working as colleagues, can request observations and provide coaching to improve teaching in a safe, impersonal, and non-judgmental environment. The two professors can use this model of peer coaching to implement a new teaching technique such as Process-Oriented Guided Inquiry Learning (POGIL) to problem solve an exasperating teaching-learning situation or to provide ongoing reflective feedback to each other on teaching techniques.

Although the belief that professional educators can improve instruction by observing, giving feedback, and coaching each other is gaining widespread acceptance in schools, colleges, and universities; many still equate peer coaching with evaluation and supervision which makes it neither peer nor coaching since the definition of supervision is evaluation by a superior or one especially appointed to supervise. In this model of peer coaching, a *coach* is one who assists a colleague in the improvement of teaching with observation, feedback, and coaching. A *peer* is a colleague of similar level or rank.

THEORETICAL FRAMEWORK

The theoretical framework for developing peer coaching began with efforts to reduce the isolation of classroom teachers and reform efforts to change and improve schools by planned and gradual improvement of classroom instruction (Hargreaves & Dawe, 1989). Criteria for developing peer coaching include a professional relationship with another educator, analysis of application, provision of technical feedback, and adaptation to student learning (Murphy, 1985).

OTHER MODELS

With the models of peer coaching available in 1987 and the experience with the Program for Effective Teaching (PET) and Resident Supervisory Support for Teachers (RSST), I researched existing models and best practices to design a peer coaching model that would meet the criteria of reducing teacher isolation, improving classroom instructional strategies, build professional relationships among instructors, provide for analysis of practice, provide technical feedback, and improve student learning. The additional question arose also to provide a cost-effective and time-efficient model for peer coaching that would be easy to implement among peers. The research-adapted criteria also included bringing peer coaching to the classroom level so that instructors as professional educators could coach on a weekly basis without an extensive reliance on supervisors, scheduling, or outside experts.

BACKGROUND OF PEER COACHING:
CLINICAL SUPERVISION

The origins of modern, data-based supervisory practice began with the work of Morris Cogan (1961) of Harvard in the Newton Public Schools. He set up a structure for dialogue and teacher choice of alternative instructional strategies in a Harvard summer school program. Cogan's implementation of clinical supervision included teaching organization skills and raising the level of professionalism among new and veteran teachers.

Another focus was promulgated by Robert Goldhammer (1969) who described technical levels of skill acquisition and building relationships between supervisor and teacher. David Purpel and his colleagues believed that clinical supervision was tied to curriculum and content knowledge and encouraged group clinical supervision (Mosher & Purpel, 1972).

In addition to their congruent criteria for clinical supervision, Cogan, Goldhammer, and Purpel had a similar structure for the clinical supervision of teachers:

1. The pre-observation conference
2. The observation
3. The post-observation conference

This type of practice included a set of skills that the teacher had learned in a professional development workshop or seminar; the supervisor reviewing the plan for demonstrating the skills in a pre-observation conference, the script-taping, or running anecdotal record on every aspect of the observation of the specific skills; and a post-observation session with the supervisor telling the teacher the strengths and weaknesses in the teacher's demonstration of the skills.

With the publication of *Clinical Supervision* in 1980, Goldhammer, Anderson, and Krajewski launched a spate of professional development workshops and seminars to spread clinical supervision into districts and schools.

As a teacher in the Greensboro public schools, I participated in one such district training led by Karolyn Snyder, graduate assistant and later spouse of Robert Anderson (Snyder, 1979). After the two-day workshop on December 4 and 5, teams of clinical supervisors were trained through five cycles of observation. As a master teacher, I was observed on February 27, 1980. It was formidable to be observed by six supervisors-in-training for one lesson and afterward to be subjected to canned questions and comments by the team of six, all of whom were far removed from the classroom and the practical applications of daily teaching. Most of the teachers in the five cycles of observation felt like felons undergoing the third degree by the arresting officers. This particular form of clinical supervision was of short duration in the district.

MADELINE HUNTER'S MODEL

Madeline Hunter's integrating theory into practice (ITIP) model provided a seven-element lesson line and specifically defined skills to increase the probability for a cause-effect relationship between teaching and learning. The eight elements—select objective, task analysis, set, explanation, question, activity, respond, closure—were skills which could be learned by any novice and could be observed by a clinical supervisor who was script-taping a lesson. As this model spread to every state and to 35 countries, South Carolina adapted the model as the Program for Effective Teaching (PET).

Training cadres of clinical supervisors to provide professional development workshops in Hunter's lesson line and elements of effective teaching was the consuming charge of the leadership and school improvement section of the state department of education during my tenure. The PET clinical supervisors had the benefit of Hunter's direct words of wisdom each year, and her model of effective teaching and clinical supervision eventually reached almost every teacher in the state during the period from 1984 until 1990.

With the departure of the reform Governor Richard Riley to Washington to serve as President Bill Clinton's Secretary of Education, the conservative cuts in the state budget could not sustain the state-wide cadre of PET trainers and clinical supervisors. The widespread use of the lesson line and the elements of effective teaching long outlasted the disappearance of the clinical supervisors.

SUPERVISORS COACHING TEACHERS

Another model by Joyce and Showers (1982) was among the first to use the term *coaching* instead of clinical supervision. Transfer of a newly learned teaching skill into classroom practice was the critical attribute of Joyce and Showers' model. The coaching of teaching included designs for transferring the new knowledge, skill, concept, or behavior into daily practice. Feedback and coaching would ensure that the new skills became part of daily practice. Their later research provided the following percentages at a professional development seminar while I was a program coordinator for the South Carolina Department of Education.

The coaching of teaching model included a cadre of designated and trained supervisors to provide the coaching of teaching.

Hunter's model of clinical supervision and the model of Joyce and Showers linked professional development with the implementation of coaching. Hunter's lesson line was intended to be taught to teachers, and the clinical supervision involved an additional line of supervisors to make sure that each teacher could implement the Hunter lesson line. Joyce and Showers saw coaching as essential to the institutionalization of any new staff development model. An example of this procedure would be the outside consultants training teachers in the use of Teacher Expectations Student Achievement (TESA) and internal coaching to make sure teachers could implement the model.

CONNECTION WITH TEACHER EVALUATION

Could a clinical supervisor evolve into a coach and an evaluator of teaching? Hunter (1993) maintained that one could be a supervi-

Table 1.1. Transfer of New Learning into the Daily Practice of Teaching

	Knowledge Level or Short Term (%)	Application Level or Long Term (%)
Theory	20	5
Demonstration	35	10
Modeling and Guided Practice	70	20
Feedback	80	25
Coaching	90	90

Joyce, B., & Showers, B. (1987, January). *Professional development seminar on the coaching of teaching.* Columbia: South Carolina State Department of Education.

sor and a coach and an evaluator if all the elements of effective clinical supervision were present and supported. She decried the evolution of the effective teaching elements into merely a checklist for evaluation.

Another view was emerging, one in which the functions of the coach as the formative evaluator and the supervisor as the summative evaluator were separated (Popham, 1988). Popham was of the opinion that the authority of the evaluator could not reside in the same person who did the supportive coaching for improvement defined in formative evaluation. Popham's viewpoint was essential to the new model of peer coaching in its purest form. (See appendix 8 for a chart contrasting Hunter and Popham views.)

SCHOOL-BASED IMPLICATIONS

Extensive experience in public schools in South Carolina brought an additional question to the creation of a cost-efficient and time-effective model of peer coaching. If we kept the hierarchical evaluative function of the supervisor or principal in this model of peer coaching, would teachers end up evaluating each other? *No* had to be the answer. Experience in implementing an early model of peer coaching in the South Carolina effective schools training in 331 public schools in the state revealed that teachers did not want that peer evaluative function to judge their colleagues and that they would not implement a model that absolved the principal or supervisor of the evaluative function. If the model set up teacher peers as evaluators, the function of daily or weekly coaching for instructional improvement would be lost (Gottesman & Jennings, 1994).

Later researchers (Rogers, 1987; Popham, 1988; Poole, 1994) confirmed the value of removing the evaluative function from a developing model of peer coaching that teachers would feel comfortable using after a professional development seminar and guided practice. The "contrived collegiality" that was criticized in early models that had colleagues working together in harmony as a primary criteria was also dropped (Hargreaves & Dawe, 1980). Instead of contrived collegiality, the new model of peer coaching had a research design of an easily implemented professional development seminar: five simple steps or components, guided practice, and a schedule for implementation which allowed teachers to use the model almost immediately on their own.

This model of peer coaching was intended as a primer: first steps in teacher-to-teacher peer coaching without the extensive training and whole-school reform required for cognitive coaching (Costa & Garmston, 1994) or the cost and time for a second line of supervisors to be trained to coach teachers.

The study involved the development and implementation of peer coaching which included the following criteria from a synthesis of the research:

Reducing teacher isolation.
Improving classroom instructional strategies.
Building professional relationships among teachers.
Providing for analysis of practice.
Providing technical feedback.
Improving student learning (Murphy, 1985).

The criteria for developmental implementation in a state with a marginal educational budget and low per pupil expenditures:

Cost effectiveness.
Time efficient (Gottesman & Jennings, 1994).

The additional criteria from studying implementation (1986–1991) and best practices in 331 public schools in South Carolina were:

No evaluative function for teachers as peer coaches.
Short, efficient training.
Practicality for daily or weekly use.
Freedom from supervisors.
Absence of scheduling problems (Gottesman, 2000).

APPLICATIONS FOR HIGHER EDUCATION

With the successful implementation of peer coaching in many comprehensive staff development programs and implementation in elementary, middle, and high schools, I turned my attention to applications at the college and university level. These applications began in the early nineties with a triad program at the University of South Carolina at Aiken and at Columbia College with the education faculty and the arts and sciences faculty leading the way.

In the early years of the 21st century, I applied peer coaching at the graduate level in the master's program at San José State University. During this time, I also translated the theory into practice for one national network for university chemistry professors who were implementing a new teaching technique. At Virginia Commonwealth University, I provided the necessary implementation skills to the faculty. With the University of Alaska's Anchorage campus and its far-flung branches, peer coaching was implemented locally and via technology between teaching partners at a distance in an adaptation called "Colleague to Colleague."

This model for higher education instructors and professors comes from school-based research and practice and also from successful application at the graduate and undergraduate levels of university teaching.

The structure for this book includes the rules, the theory, and the practice of implementing peer coaching between two teachers at the university level. Peer coaching partners are referred to throughout as *teachers*: the requesting teacher and the coaching teacher. This model emphasizes the act of teaching at any level with special attention to the implementation of any particular technique that the faculty wishes to develop among the teaching faculty by using peer coaching to implement and improve the specific technique.

SUMMARY

The book provides the theory and development of peer coaching. Theory into practice with the specific rules of peer coaching are clearly listed and detailed. Some logical and psychological reasons for why peer coaching works answer many questions by professors and others. Six examples of the application of peer coaching at universities and colleges are provided. One aspect of peer coaching is highlighted in each application example. The last chapter provides a summary and applications about the practicality of using peer coaching in higher education. Appendices include detailed guidelines for peer coaching exchanges, the debriefing questions, active listening, an outline for a faculty development seminar, handouts for a faculty seminar, and examples of actual peer coaching exchanges.

2

THEORY IN USE

Concepts and Rules

If we agree that the nature of the relationships among adults in the school learning community is one of the factors that results in student success (Barth, 1990), then creating a model for professional development that provides a structure for teachers to talk with peers and analyze lessons might also become a factor in student success.

This model of peer coaching provides a structure of simple procedures and rules for teachers to begin the conversation about instructional strategies in a non-threatening manner and also includes a structure to begin lesson analysis without evaluation. Teachers conversing with teachers on an equal level about professional analysis of a lesson increases teacher professionalism in a way that a supervisor coaching a teacher could not so easily do. In most cases, the supervisor is *telling* the teacher, not giving feedback and coaching.

Empowerment of teachers in improving their own instructional practice is a primary aim of this model of peer coaching. In this model, each teacher has the power to request that another teacher coach him or her.

In this model, the teacher who coaches has the power to give feedback and suggestions, not to evaluate. Teachers who assume the power to discuss their own instructional strategies on a professional level are joining the recognized professions such as doctors and others. Doctors diagnosing medical problems or performing operations frequently consult with their peers to improve their diagnostic ability and the procedures involved in an operation. They are professionals seeking the feedback and advice of another professional in the field.

Teachers who have a safe, organized structure to talk about instructional improvement are more likely to improve their practice. Teachers who feel comfortable with a structured and simple set of procedures are more likely to use the model than a model which requires extensive training, a second line of supervisors, and scheduling problems. Many of the best innovations of the 20th century school reform movements failed, not because they were bad models; but because they were not institutionalized (Sarason, 1991). During the seventies, researchers found that as few as 10 percent of staff development participants implemented what they had learned (Showers & Joyce, 1996).

The critical elements for transfer from the staff development training to use in the classroom are present in the one-day seminar for peer coaching: Theory, Demonstration, Modeling and Guided Practice, Feedback, and Coaching (Showers & Joyce, 1984).

THEORY INTO PRACTICE: RULES FOR PEER COACHING

Peer coaching involves five simple steps or components with a suggested time limit for each step. The process should take place within one school day, with the request for a visit taking place previously as desired.

Five Components or Steps

1. Requesting a Visit for Problem Solving. (5 minutes)
2. The Visit. (10 minutes)
3. Reflecting Alone: the coaching teacher reviews the data collection and notes and lists some possibilities for improvement. (10 to 15 minutes)

4. Reflecting Together: the coaching teacher presents the data collection and the notes as feedback to the requesting teacher and prompts analysis of the problem. If the requesting teacher is ready for real coaching, the coach lists the suggestions for improvement. (10 minutes)
5. Debriefing: Did the process work? Was the data gathering method the most effective? (3 minutes)

Some Possibilities for Peer Coaching Requests

1. Teacher questions, student responses, teacher follow-up.
2. Handedness—teaching to right or left side, ignoring other students.
3. Proximity—teacher movements indicated by arrows on seating chart or a sociogram.
4. Wait time.
5. Male-female pattern of responses.
6. Ethnicity patterns of responses.
7. Learner responses.
8. Positive/negative statements by recording all statements.
9. Praise/praise of learning.
10. Kinds of reinforcement of correct and incorrect responses.
11. All questions—the requesting teacher in step 4, Reflecting Together, identifies levels of Bloom's taxonomy.
12. Interaction with one student or one group.
13. Time spent on materials, directions, or non-instructional talk.
14. Material management and traffic flow.
15. Student movement.
16. List of teacher's non-content statements.
17. Teacher's disciplinary comments.
18. Opening set or focus.
19. Closure or summary statement.
20. Statement of objective.
21. Question first or name first?

22. Clear explanation: list all steps or points.
23. Student-to-student responses.
24. Closing 10 minutes of class: student summary, teacher summary, sharing.
25. Homework, research or project directions.
26. Teacher talk time versus student learning or guided practice time.

A CHECKLIST FOR THE FIVE COMPONENTS WITH MAXIMUM TIMES

1. Requesting a Visit for Problem Solving (5 minutes)
   __ Observation requested
   __ Specific concern defined
   __ Coaching teacher narrows concern
   __ Confidentiality established
   __ No judgment or evaluation
   __ Lesson to be observed
   __ Data-gathering method, both decide
   __ Seating chart, if necessary
   __ Observer-coaching teacher seating or placement
   __ Time/place
   __ Time for step 5
   Notes:
2. Visit (10 minutes)
   __ Request written at top of page as reminder
   __ Starting/ending time
   __ Method to be used to collect data
   __ Data collection on separate sheet
   __ No judgment or evaluation
   Notes:
3. Reflecting Alone: the coaching teacher reviews notes and lists some possibilities for suggestions for improvement if the requesting teacher is ready

__ Coaching teacher reviews data, deletes evaluative or judgmental comments

__ Feedback and coaching is based *only* on the written data collected

__ Three leading questions listed on Coaching Form # 1

__ No judgment or evaluation

__ Suggestions listed on Coaching Form # 2

Notes:

4. Reflecting Together: The coaching teacher presents the data gathered by the agreed-upon methods, prompts the requesting teacher to self-analysis, and provides suggestions for improvement when the requesting teacher is ready to assimilate them (5–10 minutes)

__ Plan where to sit in relation to requesting teacher

__ Requesting teacher or coaching teacher restatement of request in order to begin

__ Stay away from "I" messages

__ Coaching teacher goes over specific written data collected and makes no outside observations, sharing notes between the two of them

__ Coaching teacher careful not to be trapped by requesting teacher's comments "What did you think of my lesson?"

__ Ask three leading questions to analyze data collected on the specific concern

__ Teacher analysis: get the requesting teacher to do the talking

__ No judgment or evaluation

__ Teacher request for coaching suggestions or alternatives

__ Teacher request for further observation

__ Coaching teacher gives requesting teacher all notes or tapes

__ Schedule another session or exchange

Notes:

5. Debriefing: Did the process work for us? (3 minutes)

__ Requesting teacher's reaction to observation/coaching

__ Coaching teacher's reaction to observation/coaching

__ Value of chosen data collection method
__ Conference strengths and weaknesses
__ 14 Process Review Questions
__ Who learned the most?
__ Next session?

Table 2.1. Coaching Form # 1

Request for Visit:

_____

_____

Leading Questions:
1.
_____

2.
_____

3.
_____

-------------------------------cut here and separate forms----------------------------------

Coaching Form # 2

Suggestions for changes or improvements when the teacher requests them:
1.
_____

2.
_____

3.
_____

_____

PEER COACHING: THREE PHASES

If the faculty members are hesitant about plunging directly into coaching in pairs, this time table will help them ease into it. The first simple steps include watching another teacher teach with no comments. With this timetable, the faculty could progress to real peer coaching in graduated steps.

I. Peer watching (2 months)
  A. Four visits to another classroom
    1. Noted on record
    2. No feedback
  B. Videotapes of self
    1. Four lessons taped and watched
    2. Four tapes erased
II. Peer feedback (2 months)
  A. Training session: Five steps of peer coaching
  B. Coach offers no suggestions
  C. Four feedback sessions with peer with no suggestions, just feedback of data
III. Peer coaching (2 months)
  A. Review of five steps
  B. Coach offers suggestions when asked
  C. Four visits and four true peer coaching exchanges

POINTS FROM THOMAS GORDON'S ACTIVE LISTENING

1. Avoid ordering, directing, commanding.
2. Avoid warning, admonishing, moralizing, preaching.
3. Avoid advising, giving solutions or suggestions.
4. Avoid lecturing, teaching, giving logical examples.
5. Avoid judging, criticizing.
6. Avoid disagreeing, blaming.
7. Avoid praising, agreeing.
8. Avoid name-calling, ridiculing, shaming.

Table 2.2. Peer Coaching Exchange

Month 1	Four sessions	Teacher	Teacher
Dates:			
Month 2	Four sessions	Teacher	Teacher
Dates:			
Notes:			
Most beneficial:			
Barriers encountered:			

9. Avoid interpreting, analyzing, diagnosing.
10. Avoid reassuring, sympathizing, consoling, supporting.
11. Avoid probing, questioning, interrogating.
12. Avoid withdrawing, distracting, humoring, diverting (Gordon, 1977).

For further study, consult Steve Covey's empathic listening in *Seven Habits of Highly Effective People* (1989).

PEER COACHING: DOS AND DON'TS

Dos

1. Listen actively.
2. Pause . . . and make reflective statements.

3. Insert neutral probing questions to get the peer to continue reflection.
4. Bite your tongue . . . and let the teacher talk.
5. Let the peer fill the silent gaps.
6. Review only the written data.
7. Leave other concerns for another visit.
8. Refer to the safety of the peer coaching rules.
9. Offer to gather data using a different method.
10. Lead into another visit or exchange.

Don'ts

1. Praise.
2. Blame.
3. Judge.
4. Set yourself as an example.
5. Offer solutions on your own not supported by research or practice.
6. Talk before an adequate pause to get the other person going.
7. Offer data that is not written as observed.
8. Examine concerns that were not requested: offer no sidelines.
9. Offer to break the peer coaching rules.
10. No praise, no blame: worth repeating.

SUMMARY

The rigid rules for the practical application of peer coaching in colleges and universities are explained in detail

3

WHY IT WORKS
AND HOW

THEORY INTO PRACTICE: CONCEPTS

The research-based criteria for the effectiveness of peer coaching include:

1. Reducing teacher isolation.
2. Improving classroom instructional strategies.
3. Building professional relationships among teachers, providing for analysis of practice, providing technical feedback.
4. Improving student learning (Murphy, 1985).
5. Cost effectiveness and time efficient (Gottesman & Jennings, 1994).
6. No evaluative function for teachers as peer coaches; short, efficient training.
7. Practicality for daily or weekly use; freedom from supervisors; and absence of scheduling problems (Gottesman, 2000).

REDUCING TEACHER ISOLATION

The old definition that a college or a school is a collection of boxes of individual classrooms connected only by a common parking lot is surely fading away, but teacher isolation continues to be a concern. Some teachers say that they would prefer to close their doors and teach students in the old tried and true methods alone. One wonders about an adult who would prefer being alone constantly with students behind closed doors instead of welcoming interaction with other adults on improving their professional practice to help students succeed.

Interaction with other professional educators can set up networks for instructional improvement and increase the professionalism of what is sometimes called the non-profession of teaching since we should regulate ourselves instead of being subjected to outside regulations.

Star Trek introductions proclaim space as the final frontier, but many researchers (Minsky, 1985; Caine & Caine, 1991; Sylwester, 1995; Marzano, 2003) believe, as do many educators, that the human brain and how it processes information constitutes the final frontier. I frequently use the introduction of arithmetic to point out the value of collaborating with the many minds of professional educators in order to improve practice and ensure the success of students. In a seminar with 31 teachers, each teacher was asked to list the number of years as a professional educator and then total the years in each learning team (small group). The seminar total of 643 years as professional educators is a huge repository of experience, learning, and practicality upon which to draw. Certainly that vast repository of human experience and practical application of what works and does not work is more valuable than one mind of one teacher behind a closed door not interacting with other adults in the school.

This model of peer coaching provides a simple, structured process to help teachers begin to use their vast experience and practical applications to help each other at the level of daily classroom experience. This model does not offer peer coaching as the final answer that consultants and evaluators and more extensive training can offer, but it does outline a place to begin.

The traditional procedures such as pre-observation conference, observation, and post-observation conference are transformed into more user-friendly, professional educator steps:

1. Requesting a Visit.
2. The Visit.
3. Reflecting Alone.
4. Reflecting Together.
5. Debriefing.

The one-day seminar for introducing peer coaching to teachers provides the simple rules and procedures as well as guided practice in feedback and coaching.

PROVIDING FOR ANALYSIS OF PRACTICE

This model of peer coaching places the initiative in the hands of the teacher who becomes the professional educator seeking a solution to a teaching or learning question. Unlike clinical supervision, evaluation, or some other models of peer coaching, the teacher is not subject to an announced or unannounced observation by the department head making the one visit to the class for promotion and tenure purposes. Unlike this one-time visit, a coaching exchange between peers can be used on a daily or weekly basis for teachers to observe and give feedback to each other. It can also be used to document in the tenure dossier the instructor's efforts at collaborative learning to improve the act of teaching.

The psychological basis for the success of this model rest on:

1. Building trust between coaching pairs.
2. Following the peer coaching rules as a safety net to avoid personal issues.
3. Resisting the urge to *tell* rather than to promote discussion.
4. Progressing from simple watching to coaching suggestions when the requesting teacher is ready.
5. No praise, no blame—just discussion between professionals.

After instructors engage in a three- or four-hour seminar (described in appendix 4) to learn the simple rules of this model of peer coaching, instructors seek partners among the group. Pairs of teachers call upon each other for classroom observations in a simple step called the Request for a Visit. Until the pairs feel comfortable with each other, the first exchanges should be just visiting the classroom, observing, and making no comments or feedback. For most teachers in their customary isolation, this is a very necessary first step.

After the peer coaching partners have exchanged a few simple classroom visits, they are ready for the next steps. The teacher who is seeking coaching states the problem in teaching or learning or asks for feedback on a new technique or program he or she is implementing. The requesting teacher and the coaching teacher discuss the data-gathering method, note taking, tally, or other written device for recording the observation. The coach observes, records, and provides feedback *only* upon the request. Because the focus is narrow for one observation, feedback can be specific. Because peer coaches eschew any evaluative function, no evaluation or judgment can be present in the feedback from an observation or visit.

The coach, using the agreed-upon written data collection method, acts as an extra set of ears and eyes to give the teacher another focus or a more realistic view of the teaching-learning process taking place in the classroom than any person can see by himself or herself alone. In the feedback stage, the coach simply uses the data collection method and relates what he or she saw with no judgment or evaluation attached.

In the third phase of this model of peer coaching, the coach can add suggestions for improvement once the requesting teacher finds a comfort level with someone else in the classroom and simple feedback. Destruction of the process and failure of peer coaching can occur if the coach rushes or forces the suggestions for improvement before the comfort level of the requesting teacher is reached with simple observation or simple feedback.

Our instinct has been conditioned to say something positive or to give a "warm fuzzy" before the real evaluative comments. Since this peer coaching is not supervision or evaluation, irrelevant positive or negative comments are strictly prohibited: No praise, no blame. At the critical step 4, Reflecting Together, great care is taken to plunge directly into the request for coaching. This is a great time saver and preserves the focus.

There is a great difference between beginning in step 4 with a positive generalized comment and beginning step 4 with a simple restatement of the coaching request. The difference between starting the step with a comment such as "The general atmosphere was one of Socratic exchange" veers off the point. A statement such as "Remember you asked me to observe and record student answers to questions" leads to more fruitful discussions about how the teacher can improve his or her questioning techniques, how to raise the level of student responses, and how to distribute questions among the whole range of learning abilities in the class.

The second scenario by the coach is the more professional way to direct the conversation into teaching-learning techniques instead of personal praise or blame which is usually irrelevant. There is a place for praise or blame in a department chair's evaluation, but not here in coaching exchanges between two peers.

IMPROVING CLASSROOM INSTRUCTIONAL STRATEGIES

If teachers are isolated in classrooms and have no outside view of their instructional practices except for the observation for promotion and tenure, it is very difficult to analyze what is working for student learning, to change instructional strategies, and to improve possibilities for student learning. Building trust and confidentiality between coaching partners is essential to this process. Partners may continue to coach each other for months, but spreading the process by the grass roots method is almost revolutionary. Each of the original partners can take a new partner in the peer coaching process and build another trust relationship for the improvement of teaching.

After some months with the new coaching partner, each of the four takes a new partner, builds a new trust relationship, and spreads the fire like cell division at the grass roots level. Imagine a whole department of 32 faculty members using peer coaching with the simple process beginning with two partners, then four in the process, leading to eight, sixteen, and finally thirty-two. As Margaret Mead said, "Never doubt that a small group of thoughtful committed people can change the world: indeed it's the only thing that ever has."

One of the most successful models of coaching at a more advanced stage is video taping a lesson from each teacher in the department and later gathering as a group to analyze and discuss strategies after all have viewed the taped lesson (Rogers, 1987). This advanced stage cannot be lightly entered into until an environment of trust and practice of giving and receiving feedback has been established in a college department or in a team specifically constituted to peer coach together.

The present model of peer coaching provides a simple structure to build trust between partners, to establish a safe practice between peers, and to institutionalize the feedback and coaching routine as a natural process in teaching. Video taping lessons, viewing the video tape as a group, and the whole department critiquing one teacher at a time takes much more practice and trust than beginning as partners and establishing peer coaching in a department, team, or school. Some have advanced to that level for their department meetings, but only after long practice between peers and a great deal of trust building.

PROVIDING TECHNICAL FEEDBACK

The two safety nets of the present model of peer coaching include the empowerment of the teacher who makes a request for the observation and the developmental stages of peer coaching from (1) simple observation, (2) observation with feedback, and (3) observation with feedback and the suggestions for improvement that constitute real coaching.

If the teacher requests an observation visit from a peer coaching partner, he or she is interested in solving a specific problem in teaching or learning or getting feedback on a new technique or strategy he or she is implementing in the classroom. The power is with the professional teacher who wants to improve. It is a sharp contrast to the clinical supervision model or the evaluation process where the department chair comes in to make a judgment on how the teacher is carrying out a required process or coming in to write a summative evaluation.

If a professional teacher requests an observation visit from a peer coaching partner, the interest in improvement is present. The expressed wish for technical feedback on a problem or a new technique presupposes that the teacher will consider and implement the advice.

Because the teacher and the coach agree upon the data-gathering device beforehand, it is more likely that the teacher can use the information to improve. At the beginning, most teachers are interested in simple tallies; interactions with students in the form of questioning, distribution, and teacher response, or sociograms which gather data on proximity. As the coaching pairs exchange visits and build trust, the requests for observation become more complex and advanced. The advanced requests include analyzing higher order questioning and assignments, progression of incremental lesson parts, wait time, and effective research assignments.

Because the structure provides for the partners deciding on the data-gathering method each time, the partners can discard any device that is inadequate, can try again if the agreed-upon device did not provide the information needed, or agree to complex data-gathering methods which will provide more information. All data gathered during the visit must be in written form so that both partners can see the evidence. The fact that the empowered partners have the peer coaching exchange in their control means that they can repeat the exchange if it does not provide the needed information, discard any inadequate data-gathering device, or do a series of peer coaching exchanges to gather accurate and progressive information. They can arrange exchanges for peer coaching to meet their own teaching days and class schedules.

IMPROVING STUDENT LEARNING

Simple axioms for this model of peer coaching are:

1. If the teacher is concerned about teaching techniques enough to ask for a peer to visit and coach, then he or she wants to improve.
2. If the coach and the teacher together discuss the data collected to analyze the problem together, both the teacher and the coach will improve.
3. If the requesting teacher and the coaching teacher improve any one part of the teaching act; the students benefit, even if it is only small, incremental improvement.

TIME EFFICIENT

The present model of peer coaching requires a one-day, three- or four-hour seminar for rationale, content, modeling, and guided practice so that all faculty who want to peer coach start from the same basis. It is very important that the faculty group involved in peer coaching adhere rigidly to the rules since they provide a safety net to avoid personal praise or blame.

The most time efficient component of peer coaching is the fact that it does not take up the whole lesson period of whatever length and require note-taking on every single aspect of a lesson. A peer coaching request is based on a specific problem in teaching or a specific observation of a new technique the teacher wishes to implement. The rules for peer coaching provide for a 10- to 15-minute observation on one specific aspect of the teaching act, not the entire lesson. Because the time for the observation is short, the process of peer coaching can be used more frequently.

The total procedure for the present model of peer coaching should take no more than an hour: 5 minutes to discuss the request and agree upon the data-gathering device, 10 to 15 minutes to observe the specific request, 10 to 15 minutes for the coach to reflect alone and pose some suggestions for improvement, 10 minutes after classes to discuss the observation and the specific request, and 5 minutes at the most to debrief the process.

The time is very short since only one specific request is observed, data is gathered on that one concern, and that one concern is analyzed. Sticking to the subject under discussion allows for a clean, specific analysis of one particular problem. No time is wasted covering the whole lesson, other issues, or beating around the bush.

NO EVALUATIVE FUNCTION FOR TEACHERS AS PEER COACHES

The motto for the present model of peer coaching is "No praise, no blame." Teachers are not evaluating each other, they are merely observing, gathering data as another pair of eyes and ears, and giving feedback to the partner. When the partner is ready for suggestions for improvement, the coach can deliver those suggestions in true peer coaching in a non-threatening and non-evaluative way.

As Popham (1988) describes it, this is the formative evaluation function of the coach, to make suggestions for improvement before the summative evaluation of the department chair.

SHORT, EFFICIENT TRAINING

The cost effectiveness of the present model of peer coaching involves a trainer or consultant or outsider versed in the use of peer coaching providing a short, simple structure which carries out the required elements of model professional development to ensure that more than 10 percent of the teachers use the model (Showers & Joyce, 1984). The critical elements for transfer from the staff development training to use in the classroom are present in the one-day seminar for peer coaching: Theory, Demonstration, Modeling and Guided Practice, Feedback, and Coaching (Showers & Joyce, 1984).

PRACTICALITY FOR DAILY OR WEEKLY USE

Because the present model of peer coaching requires no extensive training, no second line of supervisors who act as coaches and no cost or external scheduling problems, teachers can use the model on their own time, under their own control, and with the flexibility to coach when a concern or problem arises with the peer coaching partner. Many teachers coach with a partner until a level of comfort is reached and then each branches out to peer coaching exchanges with others in their department or in other departments.

SUMMARY

Peer coaching is effective in colleges and universities because it demands that partners trust each other and focus on one specific concern in each peer coaching exchange. It is time efficient because it takes less than an hour of colleagues' time. It also has the advantage of being a grass roots movement which starts with two partners and could spread to the entire teaching faculty. Even if one improvement in student learning results from each peer coaching exchange, these incremental improvements could enhance the teaching ability of all faculty members who participate. This trusting relationship between peer coaching partners in a university and the dedication to improving student learning is surely a worthwhile goal.

4

UNIVERSITY OF SOUTH CAROLINA AT AIKEN AND COLUMBIA COLLEGE

College faculty began to use peer coaching in the early nineties in two settings at the University of South Carolina at Aiken and at Columbia College in Columbia. Faculty across campus interested in innovation in teaching, in collaborative learning, or peer support met in groups to learn some basics. Faculty paired off and observed each other at least once a month. The mixture was interesting: a test and measurements professor observing a children's literature professor, a sociologist observing a physical education instructor, and a special education faculty member observing a math professor. Teacher-to-teacher peer coaching has been difficult to implement in colleges because of some professors' definition of *academic freedom* and the typical isolation with which college teachers surround themselves. It has, however, succeeded where faculty are innovative and searching for new methods to improve teaching.

Peer coaching for college professors began when I was the state site director (1991–1998) for the Goodlad Initiative in South Carolina. Five colleges (Benedict College, Columbia College, Furman University, the University of South Carolina, and Winthrop University) had formed a collaborative and were selected as the eighth national site when John Goodlad created his National Network for Educational Renewal in 1991. Each college pledged to establish professional development schools in which to place their teaching interns, and by 1998, had established 42 professional development schools. I was director of the South Carolina Center for the Advancement of Teaching and School Leadership. In this capacity, I was the state site director for the collaborative venture.

TRIAD COACHING

An Experiment

One of the first professional development schools was Pontiac Elementary where a version of triad coaching took place with my presentation of peer coaching. A college science professor who was broker or liaison with Pontiac as a professional development school taught a graduate course in conceptual science to eight Pontiac teachers at the school site on Wednesday afternoons. The college teacher modeled each new concept. On Thursday mornings, each teacher in the graduate course implemented the new concept in his or her own classroom with the teaching intern and the college teacher as coaches. Subsequently the teaching intern would teach a lesson using the concept.

Of course, a great deal more learning and modeling took place than these simple steps indicate. The classroom teacher, who had learned from the graduate science professor, put the new concept into practice in the classroom. The teaching intern learned the new concept by observing the classroom teacher's new technique. The college teacher learned to adjust his or her teaching in the graduate course by watching two implementations of his or her theories.

The Model for Education Professors

Subsequently, the triad model was implemented with full peer coaching at the University of South Carolina at Aiken with its partnership with Aiken County Schools and at Columbia College with its 10 professional development schools.

Peer coaching for triads involves a professional model of demonstrating and learning teaching strategies and classroom management which could replace the traditional college courses, if classroom teachers were willing to be partners in training teaching interns and if college teachers were willing to put their teaching skills on the line.

In the traditional model of student teaching, prospective teachers take general education courses for two years. Lecture, note-taking, and testing are the three models of teaching which future teachers learn from many general education professors. During sophomore and junior years, future teachers are assigned to field experiences, or clinicals, in which they act as teacher aides or observers. They frequently sink or swim with no real supervision, no selection of exemplary teachers, or outline of skills to learn and practice.

During junior and senior years, future teachers take methods courses; some of which are little more than "cut and paste" making of kits and games with no real experience of learning theory or learning styles. Many education professors also use the lecture-notes-test style of teaching. They may lecture on cooperative learning or discovery but seldom if ever use or model these innovations, which are common in school and college classrooms. A startling exception is one of the national network of chemistry professors who in their implementation of Process-Oriented Guided Inquiry Learning (POGIL), a research-based classroom environment which includes both discovery and learning teams. I conducted a peer coaching seminar for this group (see chapter 6).

After learning "methods" from the traditional lecture model and perhaps teaching one "mini" lesson to classmates at the end of each course and turning in a "portfolio" of cut-and-paste artifacts, future teachers are turned loose in the classroom to work for a cooperating teacher, again with few outlines of skills or advanced learning theory and with little supervision. After 12 weeks or less, the student teacher can become certified to teach in his or her own classroom.

Using peer coaching for triads as a model for educating future teachers, taking time for modeling teaching skills and assigning deliberate reflection on practice would replace clinicals and the worse features of some methods courses.

Peer coaching began at the University of South Carolina at Aiken with a one-day seminar for all education faculty. At the end of the session, faculty members agreed to pair up and try peer coaching in their own classes. A problem-solving session was later conducted with the faculty to find out what was working and what was not working. At that point, education faculty were eager to use peer coaching with teaching interns and the master classroom teachers in the local schools.

The faculty set up triads to take peer coaching into their teacher education program and into the local schools for the student teaching experience. A triad consisted of (1) arts and sciences professor in the teaching intern's content area or the education professor who taught methods in the content area, (2) the teaching intern, and (3) the master classroom teacher in the cooperating school. At the school level, I conducted the one-day seminar in peer coaching with the master teachers who requested a teaching intern. Peer coaching for the teaching interns in this project became part of the methods courses.

In learning to teach science, for instance, the future teacher studied content and a vast repertoire of techniques for teaching science: cooperative learning, learning styles, discovery, discussion, lecture, experimentation, community projects, technological applications, and Internet research. The courses were taught on site at the local schools. Local schools that were partners with the Center for School Leadership or the Goodlad Collaborative Professional Development Schools were the preferred sites because each had built a previous trusting relationship between the university and the school. Classes on site also ensured that the teaching interns developed familiarity with lab equipment typical of public schools and that they learned practical skills from the master teachers in the classroom and from the university methods teachers.

The triad—master classroom teacher, teaching intern, and college professor—met to discuss each new concept as it was introduced. The classroom teacher would model-teach the concept to demonstrate expertise in the particular teaching technique while the college professor and the teaching intern observed and coached afterward. On the next concept, the college professor would demonstrate his or her teaching skill in the school classroom with real students while the classroom teacher and the teaching intern observed and coached. Next the teaching intern would teach the next concept to real class with the college professor and the classroom teacher observing and coaching afterward. After each concept was taught, the three people in the triad would reflect and discuss each lesson, using the rules of peer coaching.

Many college professors and master classroom teachers alike were hesitant to allow teaching interns to coach them. All soon learned that as professional colleagues following the safe and rigid rules of peer coaching, these coaching exchanges could benefit all three partners.

Like the pairs in true peer coaching, each member of the triad could learn from one another to improve his or her own teaching skills. It was interesting to observe teaching interns model a lesson and being coached. It was even more interesting to see even a master teacher model a concept and submit to coaching from a "peer" here defined as the college professor and the teaching intern. It was even rarer to see a college professor teach a concept in a public school classroom and then sit down as an equal with the classroom teacher and the teaching intern to be coached. But why not? If all three adhere to the rules of peer coaching, observe the "No praise, no blame" motto, and act like professional educators, each and all could improve his or her teaching skills and the learning of present and future students.

The additional benefit of an education professor using triad peer coaching for supervising interns is that he or she can take effective teaching skills back to his or her methods courses. An education department which also includes peer coaching as training for its teacher and principal interns can also benefit. (See chapter 8 on peer coaching as a requirement for principals and school leaders in the graduate program at San José State University.)

Arts and sciences professors also participated in the faculty use of peer coaching and developed a relationship with the local schools.

Several professors set up chat lines with local teachers in the same content area so that teachers with particular problems in science could e-mail the college professor in the content area and get immediate answers for their classrooms.

At Columbia College from 1995 to 1998, when I became department chair for education, the triad model was implemented in all 10 of Columbia College's professional development schools. College courses in methods and content areas were taught on site by education faculty and arts and sciences faculty to such an extent that students became accustomed to having many teachers and teaching interns in their classrooms.

I also instituted team teaching for these courses with an expert classroom teacher and a college faculty member. This true integration of theory and practice improved both college and local school teaching. In one instance, I asked a small child which of two tall men taught in their fourth grade classroom. When the reply was both, it was apparent that team teaching in practice matched team teaching in theory because one was the school principal and the second was the college education professor. The teacher was the third adult in the classroom.

Peer coaching, learning styles, and other professional development seminars were offered to the partner public school teachers. These succeeded so well that the vice president at Columbia College began to see the value of such professional development for college faculty. I was invited to deliver the learning styles model to all college faculty and was pleased to see its implementation in many college classrooms. Peer coaching and peer support groups became the standard across departments at Columbia College to support what faculty had learned in the learning styles seminar. Each candidate for tenure and promotion was required to document peer coaching exchanges or participation in a peer support group in his or her dossier for tenure and promotion. Thus it was institutionalized.

This partnership among education faculty, arts and sciences faculty, local school teachers, and teaching interns led to some interesting problem solving. The high school offered its labs and equipment when the college science building was under construction. The college and high school science department wrote joint grants which were funded to the greater benefit of both.

SUMMARY

While peer coaching works best in pairs, triad peer coaching or even group peer coaching (Rogers, 1987) can be adapted for interested parties who are professionals and open minded about the possibilities. It poses a new model for supervising student teaching interns where both the master classroom teacher and the college supervising professor can demonstrate teaching skills to the teaching intern. The resulting impersonal, non-evaluative peer coaching can build the skills of all three categories of teachers.

A classroom teacher can demonstrate a lesson with the teaching intern taking notes in a structured way to both coach and learn from the master teacher. The college supervising professor can learn teaching skills that work in the modern classroom and can then incorporate these new skills into his or her methods classes. The teaching intern can receive structured, constructive feedback and coaching that will directly focus on specific problems. With even an incremental improvement in teaching skills on the part of the teaching intern, the master teacher, or the college supervisor, all students benefit.

A NATIONAL
NETWORK OF
CHEMISTRY
PROFESSORS

Dr. Edward J. Baum, a chemistry professor at Grand Valley State University and the director for the Center for Excellence in Science and Mathematics Education, decided to hold a peer coaching workshop for professors in a national network of chemistry professors for some help in implementing a new chemistry teaching method called Process-Oriented Guided Inquiry Learning (POGIL).

POGIL is a research-based learning environment in which students are actively engaged in mastering course content and in developing essential skills by working in self-managed teams on guided inquiry activities. In addition to learning, understanding, and applying new concepts, students also develop important process skills in the areas of information processing, critical thinking, problem solving, teamwork, communication, management, and assessment. The instructor facilitates student learning by appropriately guiding and questioning the teams as they work through the specially designed activities. As of 2007, over 700 instructors have adopted a POGIL approach in their high school, college, and university classrooms and laboratories. (See www.pogil.org for more information.)

Dr. Baum had read my book on peer coaching and knew the process could be adapted for university and college chemistry teachers. In actuality, the process of peer coaching is best used when a group of teachers wishes to implement a new process in the teaching-learning act. It can certainly be used to solve problems in the classroom, but what better use to ensure the implementation of a new process than to have peers coach each other? Many faculty development programs wither and die after an exciting introduction or adoption because faculty have no way to ensure that their practice stays on target.

Peer coaching rules and processes can be adapted to any subject that is taught and to any management practice. The innovative program is taught to faculty; the peer coaching process is taught to faculty; and as a result, faculty have tools for observing teaching using POGIL (the new teaching technique), solving problems, and ensuring best practice among themselves.

The three components work together to provide the best implementation of any newly adopted faculty development program:

1. New program or process.
2. Peer coaching seminar.
3. Peer coaching partners coach each other on each concept and technique in the new program or process.

The workshop was planned for 42 chemistry professors from colleges and universities across the country. The site was Grand Valley State University in Allendale, Michigan, at Dr. Baum's Center for Excellence in Science and Mathematics Education, founded in 2004.

The initial concern was that peer coaching could not be adapted to the needs of college chemistry professors since it had been used mostly in high schools, middle schools, and elementary schools. Dr. Baum viewed the structure of peer coaching as applicable to any subject matter at any level as did I. The rules of this model of peer coaching are neutral and apply to any teaching situation at any level, and in fact, to other business models which require an observation of the process and feedback from the observer, such as managers coaching managers, or a mentoring program.

The five components of any peer coaching exchange are basically the same:

1. Requesting a Visit.
2. The Visit.

3. Reflecting Alone.
4. Reflecting Together.
5. Debriefing.

Each of the five components is neutral and can be applied to a college chemistry classroom as well as to an elementary science class. All the teacher has to do is to decide the aspect or problem in teaching and learning for which he wants coaching. Or the group of teachers can decide to coach each other as partners in a new process or program they wish to implement. If a new staff development or faculty development program has been chosen by the teachers or imposed upon them, each part of the new program or process can be coached. Each teacher may decide to request coaching on problems in the new program as they arise, or the group of teachers might decide to be coached on the same aspect each week, using one component of the new program each week as the peer coaching exchange.

This was the case with the chemistry professors and their new teaching techniques based on POGIL. The network of college chemistry professors was interested in finding a structure which could enable them to implement their new program more effectively and to observe and coach each other for the improvement of the process.

POGIL, like any other new method or technique, consists of subject-specific content and process to improve the teaching of undergraduate chemistry. The reason that peer coaching can be applied to a content-specific act of teaching is that it does not deal with content. Peer coaching is observation and feedback on the act of teaching rather than on the content of teaching.

Some teachers at the upper levels have loudly proclaimed that they teach the subject matter, not the students, and pride themselves on their failure rates. Most teachers, however, wish to stimulate the learning of their specific content areas by teaching to the student and using specific techniques which have been proven to increase student learning. These teaching techniques, such as questioning at higher levels than memorization, wait time, introduction and closure, time spent telling, or facilitating teaching and learning, all fall within the observable range for peer coaching exchanges.

The techniques for POGIL include students working in small groups on specially designed guided inquiry materials. The information provided guides students with leading questions to produce their own hypotheses or conclusions, which is really the scientific method reproduced. The success of POGIL is based on research in chemistry classrooms that shows that telling does not work for most students, that an interactive learning community with small groups or teams works better than a lecture situation, and that knowledge is personal. In other words, chemistry students and students in other subjects need to construct meaning and understanding from their own interaction with the data or information, be part of a learning group, and have a teacher who is facilitator and interactor, not teller.

REQUEST FOR A VISIT

With these new teaching-learning techniques in POGIL, a chemistry professor could request coaching by a peer on any perceived problem such as

1. A sociogram indicating how much time the professor spends with each learning team.
2. Questioning techniques by the professor in small group or whole class situations.
3. Questioning to male/female students or any other contrasting groups.
4. Introduction and closure for the class activity.
5. Research assignments.
6. Professor's reaction to student answers (neutral, praise, or negative and the distribution of each kind).
7. Time for critique of hypotheses.
8. Time for discussion of results.
9. Follow up comments.

THE VISIT

When the professor requesting a coaching visit narrows his or her concern to a specific observable event or period of time, the coaching professor follows the rules of peer coaching. He or she writes down the specific request for coaching so that no distractions will occur, asks the time, place, observation position, method of recording observable data, and the time and place to reflect together after the visit. The coaching professor must be careful to remain a neutral observer and refrain from becoming involved with this exciting new way to teach chemistry.

REFLECTING ALONE

The coaching professor again merely follows the rules of peer coaching. He or she makes sure that he or she has written down the specific request for coaching and prompts himself or herself to focus only on that request in the Reflecting Together component which is the next step in which he or she will analyze the observation with his or her colleague. He or she clears his or her written record of data of any praise or blame, so that the observed facts stand alone. Should the professor who requested the visit ask for feedback on the recorded data, he or she writes down some leading questions to engage his or her colleague in a dialogue that leads to analysis of the written data. His or her leading questions might consist of: "What does the data indicate?" "What decisions can you make from the data I collected?" or "Where shall we go from this peer coaching exchange?"

REFLECTING TOGETHER

With the written data in hand, the coaching professor meets his or her colleague for this component of peer coaching. He or she adheres to the rules of peer coaching as a safety net. He or she begins the dialogue with "Remember that you asked me to observe. . . ?" He or she resists any attempt by his or her colleague to delve into judgment or evaluation, such as "What did you think of my lesson?" "I think it went very well, don't you?" or other such distractions. Keeping to the request for coaching, the coaching professor indicates the written data collected, and both professors review the data.

In order to lead his or her colleague into a neutral analysis of the data, the coaching professor starts with one of his or her leading questions. The idea is to get the colleague to do most of the talking with the coaching professor refraining from praise, blame, judgment, or evaluation.

In effect, this is the hardest part of peer coaching: to examine the written data of the requested observation without getting into personal considerations or evaluation. What makes this peer coaching work is two colleagues who professionally examine the data concerning one part of the teaching-learning process. If both people adhere rigorously to the rules of peer coaching, this neutral analysis can happen. Any deviation into personal concerns, praise, blame, judgment, or evaluation destroys the peer coaching process.

This component of peer coaching should not take more than 10 minutes. The natural conclusion for such an exchange is the coaching professor requesting to be coached on the same or a similar concern.

DEBRIEFING

When both partners are new to the process of peer coaching, they could simply answer the 14 debriefing questions together.

1. Who talked the most? Why?
2. Were there any judgments or evaluative statements made?
3. If so, how can we avoid them in the future?
4. Were feelings or recorded facts discussed?
5. Did the conference include praise or blame?

6. Was the feedback specific?
7. Did the coach's questions lead the teacher to draw conclusions?
8. Did the coach become too directive?
9. Would notes or audio recording or video recording have been better?
10. Were the facts gathered and presented in a non-evaluative manner?
11. Will the process lead to the improvement of instruction?
12. Will the teacher act as a coach?
13. Will the teacher request another observation?
14. Who—teacher or coach—benefits the most from peer coaching?

As the partners become more familiar with the process and frequently schedule peer coaching exchanges, the debriefing component becomes a question of "Did it work? Why or why not"?

WORKSHOP FOR THE NATIONAL
NETWORK OF CHEMISTRY PROFESSORS

The one-day workshop was scheduled for five hours at Dr. Baum's Center for Excellence in Science and Mathematics Education. Participants were chemistry professors from one national network who came from colleges and universities all over the country.

To simulate an actual peer coaching session, each participant chose a partner for the coaching exchanges and seated themselves together at tables. If peer coaching works, it can work with an unknown partner or with a close colleague. Each participant received a handout of the design and rules of peer coaching.

The first part of the workshop consisted of the research, background, and rules of peer coaching. Partners wondered who would teach the simulated lesson for the first peer coaching exchange. The consultant eased their concerns by teaching the simulation lesson to be coached. The participants who were playing the part of the requesting professor assumed the role of the consultant's students during step 2 (The Visit) of peer coaching. The consultant chose as the lesson an unknown and quick lesson in Chi-san-bop that would keep the participants focused since it was a math lesson with which none was familiar.

After the 10 minutes lesson simulation and with step 1 (Request for a Visit) firmly in mind, the partners resumed their roles of requesting teacher and coaching teacher and role-played steps 3, 4, and 5 (Reflecting Alone, Reflecting Together, and Debriefing). Much discussion and questioning ensued about the proper application of the rules and the human failing of becoming too personal during the coaching session. Participants were continually urged to adhere to the safety net of peer coaching rules to ensure that the lesson was professionally analyzed.

Every aspect of the components of peer coaching was discussed in detail by the chemistry professors, analyzing what part worked and what part did not work. Finally the participants were ready to do the second exchange in the workshop: the participants traded roles, with the requesting teacher becoming the coaching teacher for another lesson. The second peer coaching exchange went very smoothly since the participants had hashed out all the possibilities after the first exchange.

At the end of the seminar the question needed to be answered: How do I implement this in my situation? Chemistry professors from colleges and universities scattered across the country discussed ways to implement peer coaching at their own colleges and universities. Several decided to provide the peer coaching seminar for faculty members in their own departments using the 12-page handout provided at the seminar. Some decided that they would invite all faculty to participate since peer coaching could apply to any subject. Many wished to set up an electronic exchange so they could practice coaching with a workshop participant. Video conferencing was possible for some who could not easily close the distances otherwise. The consultant's e-mail address was provided for problem solving.

Can a national network of chemistry professors use peer coaching to help each other implement their new faculty development program for teaching chemistry using POGIL? It depends entirely on how they themselves implement peer coaching as a non-evaluative, non-judgmental process for the improvement of teaching. Sharing their findings and research with colleagues in the form of expanding the partnership beyond the first two peer coaches or in the form of a workshop to share the rules and benefits of peer coaching depends upon each participant. Making decisions that will increase the professionalism of teaching by using peer coaching leads back to the 14 debriefing questions: who benefits most—the teacher or the coach? In the end, the student benefits from even an incremental improvement in the act of teaching-learning. Peer coaching can be a tool to make that happen.

DISTANCE COACHING

Long distance peer coaching exchanges between two professors who attended the Michigan seminar were also planned. Video taping, Web chat, or video conferencing can take the place of the classroom visit. Online chats or e-mail exchanges or video conferencing can provide steps 1, 4, and 5 of peer coaching. Step 3 (Reflecting Alone) is, of course, completed in the privacy of the coaching professor's office.

SUMMARY

The chemistry professors at the workshop agreed that peer coaching could be the process whereby they could observe and coach each other as they implemented POGIL, their newly adopted teaching technique for chemistry labs and lectures. Each professor was trained in POGIL and now had the components of peer coaching to use. Professors who attended the seminar with a peer from among their own faculty foresaw an easier time than those who attended solo.

Partners from the workshop planned to peer coach with each other for a month and then introduce others in their department to the rules of peer coaching. Each of the original partners would take a new partner and engage in peer coaching exchanges for a month or until the new person felt comfortable with the process. Next each of the four would take a new partner from their faculty peers within the department. Thus, peer coaching could spread by the grass roots methods that Margaret Mead so firmly encouraged.

A chemistry professor who attended the seminar as the only person from her university faced a more difficult implementation. A solo chemistry professor would have to pick a partner, induct her or him into the rules of peer coaching and practice peer coaching exchanges as partners. Taking new partners in the grass roots operation spreads the practice in the same way. Or the solo professor could provide a seminar for her or his colleagues so that all could learn the rules at the same time. Directions for conducting a faculty seminar and all the handouts were provided at the seminar and are provided in the appendices to this book.

6

VIRGINIA COMMONWEALTH UNIVERSITY

Sally Hunnicutt and Suzanne Ruder, chemistry professors at Virginia Commonwealth University (VCU) engaged in process-oriented guided inquiry learning (POGIL) and attended the peer coaching seminar in Michigan with other chemistry professors. Hearing of the success of the chemistry network peer coaching, Jeffrey S. Nugent, Director of the Center for Teaching Excellence, and Heather Williamson, director of Project Producing Results in Science and Math (PRISM) and Special Projects, at VCU invited me to conduct a seminar for all humanities and sciences faculty at VCU in August 2006.

One of the chief barriers to implementing peer coaching has been the perceived problem of coaching professors across disciplines and across age and cultural barriers. VCU professors represented a wide range of disciplines: chemistry, education, women's studies, African American studies, biology, and English. At this university, as with many other universities seeking to change faculty culture, the most successful peer coaches were those who approached the new method with an open mind, who were themselves open to new ideas, and welcomed the idea of colleagues visiting their classes.

Hunnicutt and Ruder had paved the way by engaging in peer coaching exchanges to implement and improve their use of POGIL, the new way of teaching chemistry in lecture and laboratory sessions. As has been the case in elementary, middle, and high schools, using peer coaching to implement and improve use of a new faculty development technique works best. Since peer coaching is a process applied to observation and feedback of teaching and learning techniques, it is not discipline specific. It is also easily used with the coach from one discipline and the teacher from another discipline. My first televised peer coaching exchange was playing the role of coach (with my degrees in Renaissance English literature) and the teacher being observed as a welding teacher in the vocational school in Colleton County.

In the VCU seminar for peer coaching, the participants were deliberately paired as coaching partners across disciplines. If the rules of peer coaching and the five simple steps work, they can work across disciplines and subjects as well as within the same discipline or subject.

THREE STAGES FOR CROSS-DISCIPLINE PARTNERS

Let's look at the three *stages* of peer coaching across disciplines. The first stage of partner peer coaches visiting each other's classrooms for a simple observation four times: this breaks the ice between cross-discipline partners with no risk. The second stage of visiting the classroom involves simple note-taking of the observation with feedback but no suggestions for improvement, and it gets the partners accustomed to viable note-taking strategies with no personal risk for the next four visits. The third stage of peer coaching exchanges with observation, note-taking, and feedback with real coaching or suggestions for improvement becomes a simple evolution of the process between two colleagues who have built a trusting relationship. The coaching partners can use the third stage to continue their own peer coaching exchanges, or they can use their experience to now seek other partners and spread the process in the grass roots style.

THE FIVE RULES FOR CROSS-DISCIPLINE PARTNERS

The five simple rules of peer coaching are not subject specific and pose no barrier for professors in different disciplines:

1. Request for a Visit.
2. The Visit.
3. Reflecting Alone.
4. Reflecting Together.
5. Debriefing.

In Step 1, an English professor can ask a biology professor to observe his or her classroom while he or she introduces the metaphysical poetry of John Donne. The same process is followed as when the professors are both in the same department. The specific request is to observe teacher questioning technique and student reaction during the professor's introduction to metaphysical poetry. The coach narrows the request by defining on exactly what he or she should take notes. The English professor wants the coach to write down each question he or she asks, the first student response, how the professor reacts to the student answer and/or moves on to the next student, then the next question, and a student's response. A seating chart may be helpful if the coach wishes to write down the student names. The coach will arrive at 10 a.m. on Wednesday and will sit in the back of the room. The two will meet at 2 p.m. the same day in the English professor's office to complete steps 4 and 5. They assure each other that this exchange will be in confidence and that no judgment or evaluation will take place.

Step 2, as in all peer coaching exchanges, takes place in 10 minutes to record only a sample of the English professor's questioning technique, not the entire class period. The biology professor enters, takes his or her place, records the beginning and ending time, checks the seating chart for student names, records the requested data, and departs.

In Step 3, Reflecting Alone time, the biology professor as the coach cleans up any unclear writing or notation in his or her notes. He or she is perfectly clear on the rules that feedback and coaching are based only on the written data collected, not on anything else. He or she eliminates any judgmental or evaluative statements, such as "Not enough wait time on this student." Or "No praise after this student's excellent answer." When he or she has finished reviewing notes, the coach lists three leading questions to use as probes to get the English professor talking about questioning techniques. He or she is careful to avoid *why* questions and sticks to thought-provoking leading questions, such as "What does this question and answer exchange tell you?" "What was your response to this student's incomplete answer? "When did you give the students the information they needed to answer this question: in your opening lecture, in their assigned reading, or elsewhere?"

When the peer coaching partners meet at 2 p.m. in the English professor's office in Step 4, the coach has his or her notes ready and his or her probing questions at hand on another sheet of paper. He or she and the English professor review the notes and discuss the written data collected. The coach probes with the written leading questions and leads the English professor into a self-examination of his or her questioning techniques and some conclusions. They both agree on some next steps for improvement in questioning techniques.

In Step 5, the English professor and the biology professor coach ask each other the 14 questions for debriefing or their own version of debriefing. The real question is "Did it work?" "Will improvement occur?"

1. Who talked the most? Why?
2. Were there any judgments or evaluative statements made?
3. If so, how can we avoid them in the future?
4. Were feelings or recorded facts discussed?
5. Did the conference include praise or blame?
6. Was the feedback specific?
7. Did the coach's questions lead the teacher to draw conclusions?
8. Did the coach become too directive?
9. Would notes or audio recording or video recording have been better?
10. Were the facts gathered and presented in a non-evaluative manner?
11. Will the process lead to the improvement of instruction?
12. Will the teacher act as a coach?

13. Will the teacher request another observation?
14. Who—teacher or coach—benefits the most from peer coaching?

In this particular instance, professors who were women seemed more adept at the science of data gathering and analyzing the data for coaching. Other professors might find peer coaching an invasion of privacy or the sanctity of academic freedom. The professors who were inclined to adopt peer coaching strategies were well versed in collaborative ventures and were open minded enough to know that any incremental improvement in the art and science of the teaching act would result in increased learning for students.

The end result of adopting peer coaching as an essential element in a professor's improvement in teaching skills is a more collaborative faculty. A more collaborative faculty is more inclined to seek other faculty development programs, to focus on teaching as well as scholarship, and to be concerned about student learning.

Because peer coaching has cut-and-dried rules and processes, it is easy to use and can become part of the weekly academic routine. It might even provide the basis for research into collaboration, faculty improvement, and tenacity of new techniques such as Bill Truesdale's case studies at the University of Chicago (Truesdale & Williams, 2003).

SUMMARY

One could imagine such a grass roots process spreading throughout a university. Professors in the same department would partner as peer coaches, seeking to improve student learning and their own teaching techniques. Professors from different disciplines would partner to apply peer coaching rules and use specific written data collection as the basis for impersonal feedback and coaching. The gathering of specific written data during a coaching visit could be compared to scientific data collection in the form of written notes as the scientist observes plant growth, miosis, or bacteria growth. This is not to reduce the act of teaching to observing rats in a maze; but it is to elevate the observation notes to specific observable behavior that can be recorded, to make observation a scientific examination, instead of an emotional reaction. What is recorded in writing can be discussed rather than suppositions or emotions or impressions of the act of teaching.

What does this mean for evaluations by the department head or evaluations for promotion and tenure? Peer coaching exchanges are formative, promote collegiality, and are not evaluations. Any technique, such as peer coaching, will surely be welcomed by department heads and tenure and promotion committees as a device to improve teaching, increase student success, and increase the department's reputation.

7

UNIVERSITY OF ALASKA AT ANCHORAGE

Dr. Kate O'Dell, supported by the provost, requested that we bring peer coaching to the University of Alaska at Anchorage campus in 2006. Education faculty from all branches of the University of Alaska, arts and sciences faculty, teacher leaders, and business leaders from Anchorage and the YWCA management were invited to the seminars.

The idea for this university training session was to present peer coaching in its pure, original form where *peer* means one of equal rank, not a supervisor, and *coach* means one who records data, provides feedback, and when appropriate coaches by offering suggestions for improvement. One of the major points is that the term *peer coaching* has been co-opted by many models which, in reality, does not occur between peers and involves one of higher rank *telling* instead of coaching. As a point in fact, at a Boston meeting of the Association for Supervision and Curriculum Development (one of the largest faculty development conferences in the country), a colleague and I visited 27 other sessions titled peer coaching. In none of the presentation sessions was the coaching between peers nor was it real coaching: only telling.

Professors at the University of Alaska had previously had many encounters, with largely negative results, with other models which were called peer coaching. They decided to call their adaptation of the Gottesman model "Colleague to Colleague" in order to erase all previous negative connotations. It was not the aim of the training seminar to evangelize the participants with fiery eyes to change the world in one day with the new, sensational peer coaching. It was rather a modeling and guided practice for professors and professionals to experience a new way of relating to each other. They saw it as a way for them as professionals, who care about increasing student learning, to make sure that they work daily at becoming the best teachers they can be. Dr. O'Dell called it a "Velvet Revolution," not a big, splashy reform.

This model of peer coaching does not cost extra money nor take a great deal of time. It is completely voluntary and is not required by any faculty workload agreement or faculty evaluation system. It does hold the power of any grass roots reform: beginning with two people, committed to change their practice, and spreading from the bottom upward to change the way we relate to each other as professionals. As Margaret Mead said, "Never doubt that a small group of thoughtful committed people can change the world: indeed it's the only thing that ever has."

The major barrier to overcome was the fact that another version of peer coaching had been imposed upon teachers some years previously which involved supervision, evaluation, and inadequate implementation.

To overcome both that barrier and other cultural barriers, the seminars were presented as a simple, focused business structure for observation, feedback, and eventual coaching. Again and again, the colleague-to-colleague relationship was emphasized. Neither of the partners in a peer coaching pair is superior or inferior, neither has the power to supervise, evaluate or judge her colleague. The motto of this peer coaching model is "No praise, no blame."

We can see the "no blame" part of this model of peer coaching, but why "no praise?" Simple. Both are evaluative and judgmental. If the person has the power to praise or judge that the components of the lesson were good or excellent, that makes him or her a supervisor or an evaluator. If the person has the power to blame or judge that the lesson was inadequate or inferior, that also makes him or her a supervisor or an evaluator. Thus, eliminating both praise and blame makes peer coaching a professional exchange between colleagues that depends on accurate collection of written data during the observation and the rational discussion of facts.

The five components of peer coaching were presented as a non-judgmental, non-evaluative process:

1. Requesting a Visit.
2. The Visit.
3. Reflecting Alone.
4. Reflecting Together.
5. Debriefing.

Since peer coaching is initiated by the person requesting coaching, the onerous factor of an announced faculty evaluation observation is eliminated. Two things might happen when an evaluation event is set in motion:

1. The person upon whom the observation is imposed is able to stage a showcase which may or may not show his true skills.
2. The observation notes everything that goes on without pinpointing a specific problem for solution.

The psychological advantage for having the person request a visit means that the requesting person *wants* to improve his or her performance whether he or she is a college professor, a teacher in an outlying district, or a young woman in the YWCA's leadership program. He or she is not being evaluated and is not having the observation imposed upon him or her. The advantage of the short, five-step peer coaching process is that step 1, like all the steps, takes only 5 to 10 minutes of observation within one class session and is self-initiated.

If a professor cares enough about his or her teaching style to request a visit for peer coaching, he or she is inclined to be open minded about suggestions from a colleague. That is the premise upon which this whole structure is based. As a professor sees a particular challenge in teaching, he or she calls upon a colleague for a visit for observation. The colleague as coach or the initiating professor as the teacher must narrow the concern so that it can be observed within 10 minutes. That entails setting a specific time to observe the class. If questioning techniques are the request for observation, the professor defines the visit for a specific 10 minutes when he or she plans to question students. For less class disruption, he or she can specify that his coach enter at the beginning of the class and only record data during a 10 minute period when he or she is asking questions of students. Like all good scientific data, this time sample of questioning techniques should be typical of all questioning techniques which the professor uses.

If the visit is approached in a logical manner with the coach merely gathering written facts during the visit, then two colleagues can approach the discussion in an impersonal manner. That is the reason for the rather rigid rules of this peer coaching model. The written data collection is a record of actual words said, actual observable occurrences, and actual movements within the class. There is no room for personal observations, emotions, or feelings. "Just the facts, ma'am," as Jack Webb used to say on one of the first television cop shows, *Dragnet*. Once a coach or the observed professor adds emotions, feelings, or personal statements, the whole purpose of peer coaching is destroyed.

"Just the facts, ma'am" is a good rule to be observed as the coach reflects alone to review his or her notes and to come up with some probing questions and some suggestions for improvement. If at anytime, the coach plans to say something like, "At this point, I feel that you were not questioning enough females," this peer coaching exchange is doomed! Feelings have no place in recording the observed facts in written form.

Written form leads to another barrier in a faculty development session for peer coaching. Many times when conducting this seminar, I have emphasized in the first guided practice that the coach *must* take notes in writing in order to complete the guided practice. It is impossible to do the step 3 if the coach has nothing in writing at which to look. Yet many professors playing the role of coach in the first guided practice will come back to the partner and begin step

4 with no written notes in hand. When asked by the partner or the seminar leader how they intend to discuss facts with no facts written down, most will say that they remember what happened and they *feel* they can offer suggestions or solve the teaching problem.

That is wrong and destroys the whole concept. Only by collecting written data during the observation will the peer coaching partners have written facts to discuss. It is strange that our logic applies when discussing the scientific method with students but lapses when we should apply it to ourselves.

The coach should also be careful in planning his or her probing questions and suggestions for improvement to avoid falling into the trap of beginning statements with "I feel. . . ." Rather the coach should be able to point to a written fact and say, for instance: "What was the student response when you asked this question?" With both partners looking at the written facts of the teacher question and student response, a much more logical discussion can occur.

When the professor being coached can see that his colleague is not trying to "gotcha" him or her or catch him or her in some kind of competition, he or she is more likely to be open to suggestions for improvement. In a peer coaching exchange, as in any psychologically sound discussion, the coach should avoid sending "I" messages. He or she should rather preface his or her discussion of the written fact with "you" messages. For instance she should say "At this point, you . . . " instead of saying "I think at this point. . . ."

At this point, it is helpful to remind participants of Thomas Gordon's effective listening rules and some rules gleaned from Steve Covey's *Seven Habits of Highly Effective People* (1989).

POINTS FROM THOMAS GORDON'S ACTIVE LISTENING

1. Avoid ordering, directing, commanding.
2. Avoid warning, admonishing, moralizing, preaching.
3. Avoid advising, giving solutions or suggestions.
4. Avoid lecturing, teaching, giving logical examples.
5. Avoid judging, criticizing.

6. Avoid disagreeing, blaming.
7. Avoid praising, agreeing.
8. Avoid name-calling, ridiculing, shaming.
9. Avoid interpreting, analyzing, diagnosing.
10. Avoid reassuring, sympathizing, consoling, supporting.
11. Avoid probing, questioning, interrogating.
12. Avoid withdrawing, distracting, humoring, diverting (Gordon, 1977).

For further study, consult Steve Covey's Empathic Listening in *Seven Habits of Highly Effective People.*

PEER COACHING: DOS AND DON'TS

Dos

1. Listen actively.
2. Pause . . . and make reflective statements.
3. Insert neutral probing questions to get the peer to continue reflection.
4. Bite your tongue . . . and let the teacher talk.
5. Let the peer fill the silent gaps.
6. Review only the written data.
7. Leave other concerns for another visit.
8. Refer to the safety of the peer coaching rules.
9. Offer to gather data using a different method.
10. Lead into another visit or exchange.

Don'ts

1. Praise.
2. Blame.
3. Judge.
4. Set yourself as an example.
5. Offer solutions on your own not supported by research or practice.

6. Talk before an adequate pause to get the other person going.
7. Offer data that is not written as observed.
8. Examine concerns that were not requested: offer no sidelines.
9. Offer to break the peer coaching rules.
10. No praise, no blame: worth repeating.

Perhaps it is impossible to be the perfect listener or to use all these rules as coach, but it is certainly worth a try. One of the techniques used in the training seminar in the first guided practice is to have the professor requesting the coaching to tempt the coach into breaking the rules of peer coaching. He or she is set up to begin step 4 by starting the discussion with "I feel that I did an excellent job in this lesson. Don't you agree?" When the professor starts the conversation with this ploy to get into both feelings and evaluation, it goes against the normal grain for the coach to reply with one of peer coaching's hard and fast rules: "You know I cannot offer judgment or feelings. The rules of peer coaching forbid that. Now remember that you asked me to observe. . . . Here is the data I collected in writing." If the coach has the guts to answer in that manner, then collegial peer coaching can occur.

SYMBOLS OF SUPERVISION

At this university, as with many schools and universities, it was very difficult to change the mindset of evaluation and the power of the supervisor. Many of the participants were supervisors in some capacity and were now required to remove the supervisor's hat and assume the role of colleague. As the seminar participants paired off to learn peer coaching and practice with two peer coaching exchanges, I reminded them to eliminate all the symbols of supervision for this non-evaluative model. Partners in peer coaching sit side by side as they reflect together and debrief so that they do not replicate the traditional supervisor-inferior status by seating the supervisor behind an office desk or in a teacher's desk while the inferior sits in a student desk. The coach in the peer coaching pair is not allowed to gesture with a pen or pencil as supervisors traditionally gesture to make points. The coach is not allowed to retain possession of the coaching feedback notes as an evaluating supervisor does: he or she positions the notes between his or her partner and himself or herself and leaves them with the requestor when he or she leaves. No notes or records are filed or shared with a department head or supervisor or RTP committee.

TRUST YOU?

The question of trust between equal partners in a peer coaching pair is modeled in the faculty development seminar by having them assure each other of the confidentiality of the peer coaching exchange. Repeating that assurance as part of the checklist does build trust between the partners because this model will not work if one reveals the confidential peer coaching exchange or confers with the department head or the RTP committee to reveal a colleague's teaching problems. The protocol of asking each other at every peer coaching exchange to observe trust and confidentiality is a precaution and a reminder that these exchanges are not to be shared. Strict confidentiality insures that the partners will continue to coach each other on real problems, not showcase lessons for the supervisor.

AVOIDING SHOWCASES

Will peer coaching partners always prepare a showcase lesson? This is the question which many ask. No, is the answer. If the partners are open minded and desire professional feedback on their skills, they reveal their ordinary teaching or management skills in a requested visit. If, however, the person requests a visit to showcase skills, he or she is not dealing with his or her real problems. True professionals seek to improve their skills at every level.

Master teachers more frequently request peer coaching visits. Teachers who are generally less open minded state that they need no improvement in their teaching techniques. This happens at every level. I observed peer coaching failing at an elementary school in Appalachia until the fifth grade teacher of the year asked a novice second grade teacher to coach her. Peer coaching among leadership faculty stalled at San José State University until the brilliant new faculty member, Phyllis Lindstrom, enthusiastically embraced it.

As a person who has conducted over 300 peer coaching seminars and has engaged in peer coaching in my own teaching techniques as a faculty member, department head, and national presenter since the mid-eighties, I can firmly state that once a teacher is well into the subject matter and is using his or her repertoire of teaching skills to engage the students, all intents for a showcase lesson disappear. Experienced teachers quickly get immersed in their natural state and reveal their ordinary teaching styles if they actually want to improve. It is a waste of time for a professor or any teacher to request a peer coaching visit and showcase himself or herself. A peer coach can help with improvement only if an ordinary class with the professor's daily teaching techniques is observed.

AN EQUAL PARTNERSHIP

By definition, this model of peer coaching requires that partners operate as colleagues, no matter what their status. One of the many reasons for the rather rigid rules of peer coaching is to ensure this equal status between colleagues. In the peer coaching seminar at the University of Alaska, this problem arose several times. A full professor in education could not be expected to operate as a peer coach with an adjunct faculty member who supervised student teachers . . . could she? Yes, she could. The full professor could request a visit during one of his or her methods courses from an adjunct professor who was a master teacher in the Anchorage Public Schools. Following the rigid rules of peer coaching, the two can operate as equals because the rules ensure that a completely impersonal, non-judgmental process occurs.

As the peer coaching partners participated in the first guided practice at the University of Alaska seminar, the first peer coaching exchange, they found that the rigid rules made them pay attention to what were and were not evaluative or judgmental statements. One coach told her partner that he did not call on enough female students. *Enough* is an evaluative statement. The scientific data collection during the visit portion of a peer coaching exchange demands that the coach write down teacher question, student response, and student name or sex or location on the seating chart. In the coach's notes, the teacher can see exactly which and how many female students were questioned by the teacher.

The whole group of participants discussed the nature of evaluative comments and agreed to eliminate them from peer coaching exchanges. It is very difficult to break the habits of a lifetime using evaluative comments. It makes one examine other relationships, such as parent-child. Set a standard, collect data, examine data, and discuss data. Avoiding statements such as "You don't clean your room enough" might lead to setting a standard of how often, to what degree of cleanliness, and who applies the checklist. Shall this assist in eliminating some parent-child conflicts? Or spousal discussions? We decided not to go there, to stick to the academic classroom. (However, if one is interested in this application, see Dr. Joyce Brothers [2002] "What do you think I should do?")

After a discussion about spousal coaching, participants agreed that for the purposes of collegiality in this peer coaching seminar and in their own application of peer coaching in the workplace, it would be profitable to avoid evaluative statements.

BUSINESS APPLICATIONS

For another group of participants, this adherence to the rigid rules of peer coaching was an important factor. The university had also invited downtown Anchorage business leaders to attend the seminar for university professors. Leaders in the YWCA were designing a new program for young women to develop their leadership skills. Using the rigid rules of peer coaching, it seemed that they could construct a mentoring program for an equal exchange between a Y leader and young woman in the leadership program. Coaching between these partners would not involve one teaching a lesson, but would concern an observed situation where the young woman had to apply the leadership skills she had learned in the program. The Y leaders hoped that the young women would feel less threatened in a collegial coaching situation than in the traditional supervisor evaluation model.

ACROSS DEPARTMENTS AND SUBJECT MATTER

In the training session, the professors and instructors were feeling comfortable with partners within their own disciplines or departments because they shared similar teaching experiences. In the second peer coaching exchange during the training session, the peer coaching partners looked more closely at the rigid rules for feedback and true peer coaching or offering suggestions for improvement.

The partners could follow the rules, but questioned the technique of *probing questions* to replace *telling* one's partner what to do to fix the problem. Only by asking probing questions that could apply to any teaching observation, can peer coaching cross disciplines and be applied to any subject. If a department wants to coach accuracy of content, another method is suggested. Peer coaching is an application to improve generic teaching skills.

However, content can be the subject of coaching visits if the department agrees on group peer coaching or uses video taping and group discussions outlined in Rogers (1987) "If I Can See Myself, I Can Change." Department members in Rogers' scenario must have great trust in each other and confidence in the professional discussions because their method includes video taping each colleague in turn and having each person's video as the centerpiece of a group discussion for improvement of teaching. That could get sticky in a hurry without a great deal of practice and rule-following!

Another application of group peer coaching was used at San José State University for regional groupings of school leaders to coach both content and leadership skills. A further discussion of group peer coaching is found in chapter 9 with transcripts of actual sessions in appendix 6.

DISTANCE COACHING

This university, like many, has branches all over the state. Education departments often partner with school districts in order to place teaching interns and in order to supervise those teaching interns. Both the college supervisor and the master classroom teacher working with a teaching intern can engage in peer coaching triads like those described at the University of South Carolina at Aiken and at Columbia College in South Carolina. Triads make it possible to model and coach lessons so that all three—teaching intern, college supervisor, and master classroom teacher—improve. Chapter 4 outlines this process for education departments.

The larger problem in Alaska is the great distance between branches, between schools and local education colleges, and between colleagues across departments. Peer coaching is easy to implement if both colleagues are located in the University at Anchorage. Over long distances, however, time and money do become factors.

Peer coaching works best if the partners agree to spend a day each at the partner's site. For the first exchange, one person travels in person to the partner's site; and the partners practice peer coaching in its pure form, using all five of the steps with the rigid rules. For the second exchange, the second person travels to his partner's site; and they engage in at least one in-person peer coaching exchange. As long as a trusting relationship has been built, the peer coaching exchanges can continue by means of video taping, video conferencing, online chats, Web cam or I Cam, and e-mail.

How does this work after the first in-person exchanges? The first partner requests a visit on a particular challenge in his or her teaching, perhaps the challenge he or she seeks of throwing out a question, pausing, and then calling a student name. He or she wants to change his or her technique from this less-effective practice of calling the name first and letting all the other students off the hook. He or she video tapes 10 minutes of himself or herself, using the technique where the challenge occurs, his or her questioning technique of trying to call the student name last. He or she sends the video tape to his or her colleague or perhaps embeds it on his or her webpage or via his or her Facebook site. The colleague coach reviews the video in whatever form. The coach takes written notes of the data he or she observes on the video and prepares the probing questions and suggestions for improvement. They schedule a time online for step 4 and proceed with the regular rules of peer coaching using the communication method of online chatting instead of an in-person conference. This should take no more than five to eight minutes. They debrief and schedule their next peer coaching exchange.

Admittedly this is not as good as in-person peer coaching, but it is effective if in-person exchanges have occurred first and if the partners have a trusting relationship.

Another barrier is the question of training. If you are the only person in your department or college who has participated in the one-day training seminar, how do you engage in peer coaching? There is nothing to prevent you starting a focus group to study the 12-page handout of peer coaching rules and begin the practice within your own group. Mead's admonition about a small group of committed people changing the world at the grass roots also applies to focus groups of committed, professional educators in schools, colleges, and universities. If not you, who? If not now, when? We are always looking to other research or grants to improve university teaching or teaching at any level, why not take charge of it ourselves with this simple, grass roots method?

SUMMARY

Most universities do not face the unique barriers of distance and weather that the branches of the University of Alaska do. In the education department, the barriers are doubled when education professors place teaching interns in their affiliated districts and schools which are scattered over greater distances. However, many universities have several branch campuses and teaching interns scattered across the state.

The process is the same for both:

1. A faculty development seminar in peer coaching.
2. Peer coaching exchanges by partners who attended the seminar.
3. Each pair taking new partners to continue to spread the process.
4. In-person peer coaching exchanges to start a distance relationship.
5. Electronic peer coaching exchanges via embedded video and online chats when distance is a problem.

8

SAN JOSÉ STATE
UNIVERSITY

Like most universities, San José State University (SJSU) had a well-established retention, tenure, and promotion (RTP) process. As one of the 23 state universities in the California higher education system, this university emphasized teaching over scholarship and service in its process. As a faculty member in the Educational Administration department and later as department chair for Educational Leadership, I introduced faculty peer coaching as one component of the faculty's own RTP process.

The department had a four-year graduate program for administrators and leaders in California's two-tiered administrator credential program. Since peer coaching was a requirement for graduate students in this department, it was a natural step that faculty would adopt the process to observe and coach each other.

Peer Coaching for Administrators was introduced in the initial course in the graduate program and required as an integral component for graduation in the second tier program. Since faculty were required to teach the component to their graduate students, they were very familiar with the process themselves. At the first faculty meeting of the year, each professor requested that another person in the department peer coach her or him at least once in the fall semester and at least once in the spring semester. This was a requirement for all 10 full time faculty and also for the 45 adjunct faculty who taught in San José and in the branch programs in Salinas, Santa Clara, and Santa Cruz.

The dates of the peer coaching exchanges (but not the content) were recorded as part of the RTP documentation for tenure track professors. The dates of peer coaching exchanges were also noted in the evaluation process for instructors and adjunct faculty. At times, faculty members from other departments in the College of Education were invited to peer coaching leadership faculty. The process was spread by grass roots again to other interested professors.

PEER COACHING AS AN INTEGRAL TOOL FOR GRADUATE STUDENTS

In 1999, SJSU had a two-tiered graduate program in administration certification as required by the state of California. California teachers with a credential could apply for the master's degree program and in two years, earn a master's degree and an initial administrative credential, which allowed them to seek an administrative position. In order to be employed as a principal or school administrator, the candidate then had to engage in another two-year program or a second tier in order to earn an administrative credential.

The second tier of the Educational Administration program had a peer coaching component where students were assigned across districts and sometimes at a distance to give feedback to each other on required observations in peer coaching.

When I joined the faculty, and eventually served as department chair, the program evolved to formal peer coaching as an integral part of the second tier program. I designed a shorter, more efficient second tier program which more clearly met the needs of sitting administrators, moving the program away from heavy reliance on academic class work and toward more field work which emphasized mentoring, professional coaching, and peer coaching.

Each person in the second tier program was assigned an SJSU advisor who was also a fieldwork supervisor and helped the candidate prepare an exit portfolio of competency. Each candidate also selected a district mentor.

Each candidate was assigned a peer coach from within the cohort of second tier students who was required to be on the same level but from a different district and to shadow and make site visits on a prescribed schedule.

The second tier program had a decade-long requirement for peer coaching with restrictions that at times impeded the efficacy of the main point: to provide coaching for one's peer. The restrictions upon a rigid schedule of visits, partners from widely different districts but on the same level, and regulated rules for peer feedback were lifted in favor of a theory-into-practice model which obeys the spirit of coaching without the impediments of time and distance.

Each second tier student selected an approved district mentor who could assist in promoting the candidate's career within the district. An SJSU advisor who has been a district superintendent or assistant superintendent was assigned to each student to make site visits to the student's school or district. The SJSU advisor also convened monthly meetings of his or her advisees who are grouped geographically. This small group of 10 to 15 students met with the advisor in regional meetings for group peer coaching and problem solving to further strengthen the problem solving aspects of peer coaching. Together the district mentor and the SJSU advisor constituted the candidate's professional coaching team.

THE PROFESSIONAL DEVELOPMENT ACTION PLAN

Within the cohort of second tier students, the first class sessions for the second tier established tools for self-assessment of leadership strengths and weaknesses: The Interstate School Licensure Consortium Standard's (ISSLC) *21st century Leadership Skills*; Blanchard's *Leadership Behavior Analysis II* (2001); McCarthy's *Learning Type Measure* (2000), *Hemispheric Mode Indicator* (1993), *Leadership Behavior Inventory* (1999); and Porter's *Strength Deployment Inventory*

(1992).Each candidate wrote a professional development action plan based on the assessment tools, school and district goals, and other feedback on her or his strengths and challenges for instructional leadership.

ASSESSED SKILLS AND PEER COACHING

Simultaneously with the self-assessment tools, second tier students began an analysis of Peer Coaching for Educators with the five simple steps, the safety net of rules, and the three induction phases from peer watching to peer feedback to true peer coaching. Since many of these sitting administrators were familiar with peer coaching for teachers or a similar model such as peer assisted review or beginning teacher support assistance in their own districts, the concept was not foreign to them.

Using the assessed skills, the inventoried strengths and weaknesses in their own leadership styles, feedback from the coach who was the SJSU advisor, and sparse feedback from the district mentor and district evaluations, the second tier students selected their own peer coaching partners from within the cohort of administrative candidates who took all of their classes together. The logistics of peer coaching between administrators worked best when the partners were not from the same school or district, but also worked best when the distance between partners is not too great to allow convenient monthly or bi-weekly coaching. The distance was a problem only in the beginning phase of peer coaching or if the partner requested a specific observation on a meeting, conference, or presentation.

Factors in Peer Coaching for the Cohort

The total number in the student cohort was 36, of whom 19 were female and 17 were male. The ethnic groups of this cohort were 27 Caucasian, 6 Latino, 1 African American, 1 Filipino American, and 1 Vietnamese American. Of this group, 19 were elementary school administrators, 6 were middle school, 5 were high school, 1 was an

Table 8.1. Chart of Ratings of Peer Coaching Experience

Pairings	Low	Medium	High	Total
Same school, same district	4	0	0	4
Different school, same district	2	3	7	12
Different school, different district	1	4	15	20
Total	7	7	22	36

administrator of an adult school, and 5 were district office personnel. The years as a professional educator ranged from 6 to 34 years, and the range of years as an administrator was 1 to 7 years.

The peer coaching pairing, which followed the principles of administrative peer coaching to select a partner in a different school in a different district, was used by 20 of the 36 members. For matters they deemed as greater convenience and trust, 12 chose partners in the same district but at a different school. Four (one elementary and three high school) partners insisted on a partner in the same school in the same district.

The members of the cohort rated their experiences with peer coaching at the end of the academic year. The most interesting factor was that the four who insisted on the same school in the same district pairings also rated the peer coaching experience low.

The pairings who rated their peer coaching experience consistently high were those who partnered with administrators in different schools and different districts. Comments on this pairing might indicate that those who were not afraid to reach out and try something new (different school, different district) were willing to use the rules of administrative peer coaching to learn to improve their own practice with reflective coaching and to build trust with a stranger who was committed to the same vision of excellence in leadership.

One of the key factors in leading and managing change is identified as one single item: the willingness to try something new and different (Calabrese, 2002). One of the participants, who was an assistant principal partnered with a principal in the same district at a different school insisted on the pairing because of the short distance involved; but for the final summary she regretted the choice, saying if she had to do it over again, she would choose a partner from a different district because this pairing precluded discussion of many district policies and politics.

Conversely it might be deduced from comments from the four who insisted on pairing within their own school and within their own district that high school administrators do not want to stretch out of their comfort zone to build trust with a stranger. They were also more inclined to cite time and stress factors and seem less committed to receiving feedback from peers or engaging in reflective practice on their own.

BEGINNING ADMINISTRATIVE PEER COACHING

An introduction to peer coaching for people who are administrators began with a review of Ken Blanchard's *Leadership Behavior Analysis II* (2000) in which administrators inventory and analyze their leadership behavior in varying situations and with staff on varying developmental levels on several aspects. The directive and the coaching behaviors are the two we emphasized and coupled with peer coaching for administrators. The leadership behavior strength in the coaching or non-directive style of leadership fits with the situation of coaching a peer administrator.

Comparison with Peer Coaching For Educators

A quick review of Peer Coaching for Educators established the simple five-step structure, the safety net of rules, and the three phases of watching, feedback, and coaching. The variations for administrators include following the spirit of the rules rather than the rigidity of the rules.

The concepts for peer coaching for administrators were introduced to the group as the criteria which make peer coaching for teachers successful but which also make the advanced and less location-bound coaching possible for administrators.

Shadowing

First participants learned the value of shadowing the peer coaching partner for more information about the work site and the circumstances of the partner's challenges in leadership (Berry, 1988). Coupled with a simple request for feedback, this shadowing visit could also be used for a specific observation when and if the partner wishes to be physically observed. The second principle that participants spent some time on was reflection, considered a best practice in improving teaching, learning, and leading (Barth, 1990; Sergiovanni, 1987). In this version of peer coaching, administrators, like teachers, let go of the traditional formal title of clinical supervision—post-observation conference—and act as collegial coaches to each other in segments defined as steps 3 and 4 of peer coaching.

PRELIMINARY CONCERNS

Administrators had other concerns about the efficacy of peer coaching, such as:

- Comparison of one's leadership skills with the partner's skills.
- Trust that the partner will keep strict confidentiality at all times.
- Concern about value judgments and evaluations from the partner.
- Confidence in telling teachers what to do but not in coaching a peer.

These concerns can be alleviated by imposing the rules of this model of peer coaching: no evaluation, no judgment, no praise, no blame. Engaging in trust-building exercises at the beginning and troubleshooting problems with a seminar once or twice during the year were also fruitful conversations. Pairs who were having difficulty shared with others how they built trust and solved problems.

This group peer coaching was a necessary problem-solving tactic for the successful continuation of partner peer coaching for administrators. The problem solving seminars also included a refresher on the rules of this model of peer coaching and exercises in reflective listening and feedback. Independent practice with refreshers from the advisors who were also coaches and from the program coordinator also helped keep peer coaching partners on track.

THE ONE-DAY SEMINAR TO
INTRODUCE PEER COACHING

The critical element in the success of any new program is the introduction and the first demonstration and guided practice. Peer Coaching for Administrators followed that principle with a user-friendly, practitioner-oriented one-day seminar and first practice between the partners.

A sample agenda for a seminar on Peer Coaching for Administrators:

1. Welcome and introductions.
2. Theory of peer coaching as evolved from clinical supervision and teacher evaluation.
3. Demonstration: Review of Peer Coaching for Educators.
4. Guided practice (Exercise # 1 Shadowing for peer coaching: Administrators simulation, peer watching and feedback.
   - Partner's Statement: "I am currently dealing with. . . ."
   - Shadowing: a visit to the partner's school to walk through an hour or so with the administrator as she discusses the current factors in her administrative work.
   - Feedback: the partner gives the administrator some impartial feedback on what he or she saw during the shadowing exercise or walk-through.
5. Guided practice (Exercise # 2 Administrator requests advice on problem solving).

The true peer coaching phase of administrative peer coaching follows similar steps as Peer Coaching for Educators.

- Requesting advice for problem solving.
- Site visit if necessary.
- Reflecting alone.
- Reflecting together.
- Debriefing and reflective essay for journal or log.

Partners pair off in the seminar, pose a real or simulated problem to each other, and role-play the steps in administrative peer coaching. The focus is on the probing or leading questions the coach might ask during step 4 (reflecting together). As each plays the coach in the simulation, he or she must write down during step 3 (reflecting alone) the probing questions to use for step 4.

6. Feedback and coaching: facilitators debrief participants on a Delphi chart about the strengths and weaknesses of this model.

7. Closing activity: Initial introductory conversation between peer coaching partners in order to leave the simulation and prepare for real practice.

THEORY INTO PRACTICE

The partners who are paired for administrative peer coaching had three requirements: that they shadow each other at least once on a site visit to the partner's school or district worksite, that they engage in peer coaching at least six times during the academic year, and that they keep a journal or log of peer coaching exchanges with reflective essays on the value of the peer coaching session.

Although this model had been working for three years as part of a graduate program in the second tier credential program for Educational Leadership, many districts have adopted this procedure as part of their monthly principals' meetings or their new administrators' induction programs. The same procedures and principles apply. In many districts, the role of district mentor and university advisor have been combined into the position description of a district person whose job it is to mentor and advise new administrators on a weekly basis. This is becoming more common with the rapid turnover of administrators.

The five simple steps of peer coaching have been modified for administrators and read:

1. Requesting a visit for problem solving.
2. Site visit if necessary.
3. Reflecting alone.
4. Reflecting together.
5. Debriefing and reflective essay for journal or log.

PEER COACHING FOR ADMINISTRATORS: STAGES OF IMPLEMENTATION

Initial Conversation: Trust Building and Active Listening

The first step takes place once the partners have identified themselves to each other after the introductory seminar on peer coaching. The initial conversation as the closing activity in the training seminar is the first step in building trust. This structured conversation has each of the partners speaking about himself or herself without interruption for four minutes. Each person talks about the current situation in the school, plans for the year, challenges facing him or her, resources available, plan for taking care of the inner person, and where he or she hopes to be in five years.

As each person talks for the four minutes, the partner must focus fully on the person without interruption, questions, parallel stories, or distractions.

Body language is important in this first conversation: eye contact, upright posture, no leaning forward for encouragement or leaning back with arms crossed to discourage, no frowns of disapproval, and no nods or smiles of approval.

The purpose is for each to practice fully focusing on another person. Of course, the smiles and nods come back when real life conversations take place, but it is important to over-dramatize for effect what these techniques actually accomplish. A conference can be entirely negative with lack of eye contact or leaning back with arms crossed. Four minutes seems like a long time for one person to talk without interruption, but this structured activity reveals many subtle clues to what could work better in coaching.

Each person is also aware of Gordon's rules for active listening, Covey's empathetic listening techniques, and the dos and don'ts of peer coaching.

Probing Questions

A second activity during the seminar has the focus on step 3 (reflecting alone) where the coach writes down general and specific probing questions to lead the peer coaching partner to analyze his or her own situation in step 4 (reflecting together). Administrators hate to write down probing questions because they think they can remember everything, but the quality of peer coaching is compromised if the coach tries to wing it without writing down probing questions. Many find it hard to put the mind in gear before the mouth goes into motion. This is true of most professional educators, teachers, and administrators, who spend their lives talking to a captive audience. It is very important to write down the probing questions: one can examine the written questions and meditate on them more accurately than on verbal questions that might be forgotten in the complex conversations and excitement of step 4.

Sample probing questions include open-ended questions such as:

- What triggered that idea?
- Can you tell me more about the background to this situation?
- How have you dealt with similar situations in the past?
- How did you decide to do . . . ?
- How did you plan this presentation?

- How did you decide on which aspect to tackle first?
- How did you come to that conclusion?
- What are your plans for next steps?
- What might happen if . . . ?

Avoid Questions that Begin with *Why*

Smart communicators ask questions not only so they can hear the answers, but also so the person asked can hear his or her own answers and thereby gain clarity for himself or herself or internalize something he or she has grasped only intellectually. Indeed the answers that are most effective for people are their own. Asking questions and listening to answers builds relationships among people. Questions are a gift to the person being asked, just as answers are a gift to the person asking them (Pryor, 1994).

Reflecting Together

It is important to practice this routine although administrators have participated in numerous post-observation conversations with those whom they supervise, this conversation of reflecting together with a peer coaching partner is different. The tactics of restating the request for coaching, writing down the probing questions, practicing active listening, pushing the partner to analyze, no judgment, no evaluation, no blame, no praise, all require careful consideration. Practicing these tactics with an administrator as a peer coaching partner has also been know to improve the administrator's conferences with teachers, students, and parents.

Shadowing

Visiting the partner's worksite at some point during the peer coaching cycle is necessary to have a realistic view to add to the trust building conversations between partners. The shadowing visit can reveal the partner's technique for management by walking around, daily routines, his or her relationships with people at the worksite, logistical problems, and other viewpoints that cannot be conveyed from one person's conversation.

Variations for Steps 4 and 5

It is in these two steps that the variations for administrators take place so that peer coaching may occur at some other place than strictly after a site visit on the same day at the same site. That time and place restriction has destroyed many initially promising peer coaching relationships among administrators.

Examples of informal peer coaching for administrators:

- Two administrators, both principals of elementary schools, met for an hour's walk in a nearby park on Friday afternoons, meeting three goals: relief of personal stress, leaving the office before dark, and peer coaching. One would state a problem and the other would coach while walking. Then they would reverse roles. The benefits included exercise and coaching.
- Two administrators met for lunch after the monthly district meeting and coached each other during the lunch away from school.
- Two administrators left school early to travel to a regional meeting in Gilroy. They coached each other during the two-hour travel time before and after the regional meeting
- Two high school administrators, an assistant principal and a villa principal, met for coffee once a month at Peet's Coffee, away from both their schools.

TYPICAL CYCLE OF PEER COACHING FOR ADMINISTRATORS

The timeline for the cycle of Peer Coaching for Administrators follows the timeline for the academic year.

August: Training seminar for Peer Coaching for Administrators
Partners engage in trust building initial conversations

September: First peer coaching exchange planned as shadowing the partner
Peer watching and peer feedback
October: Second exchange for problem solving
May include observation or planning
November: Third exchange for Peer Coaching for Administrators
May include observation, planning, or advice
February: Fourth exchange for Peer Coaching for Administrators
May include observation, planning, or advice
March: Fifth exchange for Peer Coaching for Administrators
May include observation, planning, or advice
April: Sixth exchange for Peer Coaching for Administrators
May include observation, planning, or advice

LOG OF PEER COACHING OR REFLECTIVE JOURNAL

An excellent professional educator is a reflective practitioner (Sergiovanni, 1987) and therefore keeps a journal for reflection on practice. In the Educational Leadership program for administrators, it was an academic requirement. It is, however, a universal good practice for administrators and teachers to write down an incident, analyze it, and decide what to do differently next time.

A simple log of the peer coaching exchanges is enough if one notes the request for coaching and the conclusions derived from the process. However, many administrators use the simple log as a reflective essay on the challenges in the school and viewpoints about the procedures to follow in solving dilemmas. A record of the problems and the decision-making process may help solve the next problem as it arises.

SUMMARY

At SJSU, peer coaching was an integral component of the graduate program for the 200 students for the Educational Leadership master's degree. Faculty in the Educational Leadership Department also observed, gave feedback, and coached each other as part of the promotion and tenure process and to improve teaching and student success within the department. Many administrators and teacher leaders who used peer coaching in their graduate program adopted it for use in their schools and districts as a faculty development process.

Because of the success of the peer coaching program for administrators, teacher leaders, district officers, and faculty development presenters, I proposed to the university administration that distance technology be used to continue peer coaching after graduation. The proposal involved using adjunct faculty as online peer coaches for graduates as they engaged in their workplaces. The same rules of peer coaching would apply online. The graduate would connect with the adjunct faculty by electronic mail and request an observation by video tape, embedded video, or video conferencing or in person. Step 4 (reflecting together) would be conducted by e-mail between the graduate and the adjunct faculty acting as coach.

Coaching after graduation could be extended to other colleges within the university. Graduates from criminal justice, library science, sciences, the arts, the humanities, social work, as well as education, could benefit from continued coaching with university professors or adjuncts concerning real workplace problems. As a student recruitment tool, this proposal appealed to many students just as the University of Georgia some years ago guaranteed its graduates or the employer could send the graduate back for retooling or additional courses.

However, the university did reject the proposal, even in the Silicon Valley of innovation and technology. Two commercial companies eventually adapted the idea successfully for life coaching.

9

GROUP PEER
COACHING TO
SOLVE PROBLEMS

Colleges and universities have adopted peer coaching for the improvement of teaching in faculties and departments. Several, especially colleges and schools of education, have adopted peer coaching as an integral part of their graduate and undergraduate programs for teachers, administrators and school leaders, and other students in mentoring programs.

An additional component for peer coaching has been developed for small groups in college or university programs. This is group peer coaching. Group peer coaching has been used successfully in the Educational Leadership graduate program to provide a common discussion group for graduate students in similar situations, districts, or regions. Individual departments who have developed a high degree of trust in regular peer coaching have also adopted this method to discuss common content, new teaching strategies, or problem areas.

Although group peer coaching is an adventure which is difficult to approach in a completely impersonal manner, it has worked well if the rules of peer coaching are applied to the group situation and the facilitator is skilled in keeping the discussion impersonal with the motto of "No praise, no blame" and reminder of "Coach, Don't Tell."

Professors and instructors familiar with other group structures will recognize some similarities with learning teams and the ideas common to small group processes. Deming's quality circles, Baldrige's learning teams, Noddings' learning communities, nominal group process, and Gottesman's participatory decision making (see appendix 7) are just a few of the small group processes developed for solving problems.

STRUCTURE

In the graduate program at San José State University for administrators, Peer Coaching for Administrators, a review of Peer Coaching for Teachers, and periodic support meeting for group coaching were part of the academic structure. After the seminar demonstrating the principles of Peer Coaching for Administrators and the immediate guided practice simulation of a coaching situation, peer coaching partners establish their own schedules of coaching. The requirement is that one of the first peer coaching exchanges include a shadowing or observation visit to the partner's work site, school, or district. Simple feedback of what the partner saw during the shadowing later leads to more specific feedback requests and coaching.

Since the service area for the graduate program was Region 5 which involves distances of up to 110 miles, participants are grouped into regional meetings sites. Participants met three times during the fall and three times during the spring to engage in group peer coaching for problem solving. Group peer coaching is based on previous experience with partner peer coaching and knowledge of the limits and challenges of that process. It also involves a greater matter of trust and confidentiality.

Research into how the brain learns drives the theory and practice of group peer coaching for problem solving. Four basic problem-solving procedures that our brains use are (1) automatic or deliberately planned solo brain operations, (2) the social orientation of temporarily borrowing the brains of others, (3) technology-enhanced problem solving with computers and reference depositories, and (4) herbal and synthetic molecules to stay awake longer or re-energize (Sylwester, 1995). Of these procedures, the second way the brain learns, the social orientation of temporarily borrowing the brains of others, is a legitimate application of brain research as the theory for the practice of group problem solving.

The applied theory of group problem solving occurs in countless management structures, theory z, quality circle, learning teams, nominal group process, participatory decision making, and the Deming and Baldrige applications of management theory that put decision making and problem solving with the team directly concerned instead of with top management.

DISTRICT APPLICATIONS

Although the academic structure for group peer coaching is part of a graduate program, any district or network of leaders can establish a structure for group peer coaching. I worked for the South Carolina state Department of Education in the late eighties when the department was one of the state partners in the United States Department of Education's Leadership in Educational Administrative Development (LEAD) Program (OERI, 1986).The OERI Director Hunter Moorman and James O. Ray in South Carolina worked closely to implement LEAD into district administrative staff development and into university administrator training programs.

One of the administrative training programs which was developed from LEAD was Peer Assisted Leadership (PAL). PAL was implemented in many districts nationally, but I worked with one in Florence School District One with Dr. John Segars in the late eighties. The program included observation, feedback, and peer support, using small group structures within the entire cadre of leaders. One of the characteristics of the Florence implementation of PAL was quarterly gatherings for principals to meet in school-level groups to help problem solve challenges in administration (OERI, 1986; Berry, 1988).Other networks may take the form of principals' study groups coupled with learning communities and peer coaching networks (Fink & Resnick, 2001). College and universities often form focus groups to solve problems, and group peer coaching is a natural application. Many businesses in the Silicon Valley are hiring coaches to lead focus groups which could also use group peer coaching.

AN EXERCISE TO ILLUSTRATE COACHING BENEFITS

This exercise is useful to provide a demonstration of the benefits of peer coaching to a small group who may not have previously engaged in a peer coaching network or for a group as an inducement before introducing the one-day seminar for peer coaching.

Uncoached and Coached Project

Materials: group in pairs   one Tangram for each pair
Blindfold for every pair   Instructions

Uncoached Segment Instructions

1. Assist your partner in securing blindfold over his or her eyes.
2. You say: "Your task is to arrange the pieces into the shape of a square, using all seven pieces."
3. Wait for the timekeeper to call time.

Important: During this part of the exercise, you are not to provide *any* assistance to your partner.

Carefully observe the approach and methods your partner uses to create the square. Begin to consider the verbal coaching techniques you might use to assist him or her in a second attempt to create a perfect square.

When time is called, do not allow your partner to remove the blindfold. Reflect with your partner on what kind of help he or she might need to assemble the pieces correctly.

The coached portion of the project begins next when time is called.

Coached Segment

Ask your partner: "Are you ready to try again with my verbal coaching?"

Repeat the instructions: "Your task is to arrange the pieces into the shape of a square, using all seven pieces."

During this coached part of the exercise, you are to provide any and all *verbal* assistance to your partner that you feel will help. He or she can also talk to you and give you feedback on whether your instructions are helping or not. Take into consideration how he or she moved the pieces during the first part of the exercise. You are not allowed to touch any of the pieces nor to guide your partner's hands in picking up or moving the pieces.

Debriefing

1. What was important in the un-coached section?
2. Did you analyze your partner's approach to problem solving in the first part of the exercise?
3. What role did vocabulary play in the second part of the exercise?
4. What did you do when your partner did not seem to be following your verbal directions?
5. Was it difficult to restrain yourself from "just doing it yourself" when your partner was having difficulty?
6. Did you find words inadequate and wish you could touch the hands or the pieces?
7. Did emotions play any part in the second part of the exercise?
8. Did you match your partner's method of assembling the pieces with your effective verbal coaching or did you just assume your partner had similar learning approaches to your own?
9. What did you learn about verbal coaching?
10. What did you learn about yourself? About teaching and learning? About assessment?

STRUCTURED GROUP PEER COACHING FOR PROBLEM SOLVING

Since trust and confidentiality are the critical attributes to the success of group peer coaching for problem solving among educators and leaders, a statement by the group facilitator or leader is essential at the beginning, middle, and end of a group peer coaching session: "Remember that what is said in this room stays here. Coaching works only in complete trust and confidentiality."

Although the peer coaching pairs have exchanged observations and feedback, it is a different ballgame to trust a group of 8 to 12 peers. However, such professional behavior and assisting each other to improve professional practice is the hallmark of taking control of one's own profession. The question arises about waiting for supervisory evaluation or new mandates from the state or taking control to improve the profession by using networks of peer coaching for educators and leaders. Who knows better than another educator what challenges arise, what district or state restrictions apply, or what people skills are needed to solve problems with teachers, students, parents, and others?

Colleges and universities can use group peer coaching as part of the evidence presented to National Council for Accreditation of Teacher Education (NCATE) evaluation teams and for other accreditation procedures which examine collegiality among the faculty. Or they may use group peer coaching to improve collegiality among faculty without the pressure of an accreditation visit.

Setting the Scene: Participants

8 to 12 persons who have had experience with the rules for peer coaching and who have had some peer coaching exchanges.

Time: Approximately 2 hours

Location: comfortable chairs around one table with no phones, laptops, or interruptions

Facilitator: one experienced in the rules for peer coaching and in peer coaching exchanges who has patience and the ability to say "Coach, don't tell" frequently.

Twelve Rules for Small Group Peer Coaching for Problem Solving

1. One person in the group states a problem, without interruption.
2. The other participants in the group listen carefully and jot down clarifying or probing questions they might ask.
3. Participants volunteer, one at a time, to ask a clarifying question or probing question of the person stating the problem. Each participant frames the question to allow the person with the problem to reflect on some aspect of the problem and think aloud about the reflection.
4. A pause after a single participant's clarifying question and the reflection and response from the person stating the problem, before the next participant asks a probing question allows time for all to reflect and ask more complex questions.
5. Each participant respects the silence for reflecting and resists the compulsion to tell his or her own experience or war stories.
6. The facilitator reminds participants of the rules of peer coaching: "Coach, don't tell" to keep the participants on track. This reminder by the facilitator happens most often in the beginning stages when groups are establishing trust. In the later stages, participants remind each other to coach, not tell.
7. This routine of each person asking a clarifying, probing or leading question, pausing, and the person stating the problem reflecting out loud continues until the person with the problem ends by saying "Thank you. You have given me some ideas."
8. The facilitator guides and limits the time for coaching for problem solving to about 20 minutes per problem. Not all

participants state a problem for group peer coaching at any one session. Some may need to build trust before exposing their challenges to the group.

9. No participant tells, judges, praises, blames, or above all says: "I remember when I had a similar situation."

10. There are no interruptions for "war stories" or discussing other people's classes or situations.

11. The mode is problem statement, leading and reflective questions, person with the problem thinking aloud.

12. Facilitator's job is to remind people to coach, not tell when they veer off the track.

Role of the Facilitator or Group Leader

The role of the facilitator for group peer coaching for problem solving works best when the leadership comes from outside the group and the leader does not participate in the problem solving. The facilitator states no problem in his or her own experience and does not offer coaching advice in the form of clarifying, probing, or leading questions. The role of the facilitator is to make the group process work, not to participate. Small groups who have used quality circles, learning teams, or participatory decision making find group peer coaching an easy evolution.

In the beginning stages of group peer coaching for problem solving, the facilitator reviews the rules for group peer coaching at the beginning of the session. The facilitator makes the statement for trust and confidentiality at the beginning, middle, and end of each session. The facilitator encourages and respects pauses for reflection and has the patience to wait in silence. The facilitator limits each problem-solving segment for each participant to about 20 minutes. The facilitator encourages participation in coaching from all group members and sets the standard for each person asking at least one clarifying or probing question. The facilitator does not insist that each participant share a problem at each session. As trust builds within the group, participants who want professional coaching from their peers will ask for it.

The role of the facilitator is not a passive role, contrary to popular opinion. Experts such as Bob Garmston (2003) outline skills, language, and procedures that "group wise" facilitators could use to become adept facilitators for any group.

SUMMARY

Group peer coaching is an adaptation of regular peer coaching for use in groups who have been trained in a peer coaching seminar, who have practiced partner peer coaching, and who have developed a high degree of trust as a cohesive unit. In order to meet challenges as a unit, the group may choose to engage in peer coaching as a group to develop common teaching techniques or to solve problems common to most of the group.

Although the rules are almost the same as in regular peer coaching, group peer coaching has some peculiar rules to ensure trust, confidentiality, and focus on the objective. In group peer coaching, a skilled facilitator and strict adherence to the rules and motto of "Coach, don't tell" and "No praise, no blame" is vital to maintain the integrity of the process. Practice with the group process participatory decision making greatly enhances group peer coaching.

10

SUMMARY AND APPLICATIONS

With the devolution of peer coaching, its developmental background, and the theory behind the process, the rigid rules in this model of peer coaching seem simple and extremely easy to use. Professors and instructors in universities and colleges will find the three phases, the five components, and the rules for each component remarkably simple.

What is not so simple is persuading oneself and one's colleagues that strict adherence to the rules in the five components is critical to the success of this peer coaching model. As professional educators are inclined to do, some professors may neglect one or several of the rules and find themselves in a highly personalized exchange with no rules to use as a safety net.

The rules have been developed in practice that now has covered two decades of application at various levels and with diverse groups of professional educators. The rule most often neglected is the one that makes this model an impersonal, non-evaluative model that anyone can use: the opening statement for step 3 (reflecting alone) must always be "Remember that you asked me to observe. . . . " When the coach can stick to the requested observation without delving into personal comments or evaluative statements, this model can succeed. When the coach succumbs to his her colleague's request for a personal, evaluative statement, the model fails.

REVIEW

A reprise of the five components and their checklists summarizes the findings from applications at five universities and two national networks with which I have been personally involved.

CHECKLIST FOR THE FIVE COMPONENTS

Requesting a Visit for Problem Solving

The professor requesting the visit or observation must be specific about what he or she wants his or her colleague to observe, collect data on, and give feedback and coaching. This should be some problem, challenge, or application which can be observed within 10 minutes. The coach can help the professor narrow the coaching concern by making sure he or she can collect written data. As in every peer coaching exchange, confidentiality is promised. No praise, no blame is the motto to avoid judgment or evaluation.

It is helpful to mention the topic of the lesson but not always necessary. It is a 10-minute sample of teaching technique which is being observed. Both professor and coach decide upon the data gathering method, as long as it is *in writing*. This is how scientists gather data on an experiment: precise facts observed, exact statements written, and a careful watch on any personal observations, judgment, or evaluation. A seating chart may be necessary if names or gender are important in the data collection. For most observations, the coach should be seated at the back of the classroom and be in place when the 10 minutes of requested observation begins. Both partners should realize the importance of step 4 (reflecting together) on the same day that the peer coaching exchange occurs.

It is more important to have many short peer coaching exchanges within the prescribed time limits than to seek solution to all teaching problems in one long observation.

What can go wrong:

- If the concern is not narrowed to what can be observed within 10 minutes, the coach will be overwhelmed with data to collect.
- If the agreed-upon data-collecting method is too cumbersome or wide ranging, precise data cannot be collected within the time frame.
- If the coach does not collect data *in written form* without extraneous comments, no material for the reflecting together session will exist.

Visit

Each coach, no matter how experienced, must write down the professor's request at the top of the page on which he or she collects data during the visit. This will focus the observation. A coach always notes the beginning and ending time for the observation as a reminder. The coach collects written data, using the agreed-upon method, and collects data on nothing other than the request for observation. The coach is careful to avoid judgment.

What can go wrong:
- If the coach writes down feelings, impressions, or emotions instead of the cold, hard facts of what he or she actually observes, true peer coaching cannot occur.
- If the coach writes down other factors such as the class environment, the noise level, or any other data besides the requested observation, peer coaching will fail.

Reflecting Alone

In this step, the coaching professor reviews notes and lists some possibilities for suggestions for improvement if the requesting professor is ready.

When the 10-minute observation is completed, the coach immediately engages in reflecting alone to prepare for talking with his or her colleague. The coach makes sure that the written data he or she has collected is clear and readable to the colleague. The coach makes sure his or her tallies, marks, and records of student names are correct. It is crucial that the coach, no matter how experienced, *write down* three leading or probing questions to prod the colleague into analyzing the lesson based on the collected, written data. It is also crucial that the coach *write down* three suggestions for improvement should the colleague be ready to ask for suggestions for improvement once the written data has been reviewed by both parties.

The coach, of course, removes any written evaluative statements or graphics, such as "Terrific." In this time-efficient and effective model, the reflecting alone time will take no more than five minutes out of a busy professor's day.

What can go wrong:
- If the coach skips this step of reflecting alone to save time, thinking that he or she can just wing it and talk with the colleague spontaneously, he or she is seriously mistaken.
- If the coach neglects to write down some probing questions to prod the colleague's self-analysis, he or she may find himself or herself telling instead of coaching.
- If the coach neglects to write down some impersonal suggestions for improvement, he or she may find herself in the role of judge or evaluator without meaning to do so.

Reflecting Together

The coach presents the data gathered by the agreed-upon methods, prompts the requesting professor to self-analysis, and provides suggestions for improvement when the requesting professor is ready to assimilate them.

It is very important that this step part takes place within the same day as the observation. Data grow cold and probing questions may lose their impact the further one gets in time from the observation. Choosing equal seating during this step part is very important for the coach to avoid the role of supervisor. The written data collection is shared on the table between the two colleagues, with each having an equal view. No pencils, pointers, or dictating fingers are in use by the coach. The coach or his or her colleague firmly restates the request for the visit, the focus of the observation. This is the only topic of conversation during this discussion. Step by step, the coach and the professor review aloud the data collected in writing.

The professor may pause for some reflection after the data is reviewed. Most professors will begin asking what the data means in relation to the originally expressed concern; but for those who do not begin on their own, the coach has his or her three probing questions ready to stimulate the conversation. The coach does not let this self-analysis drag on too long, but he or she listens carefully to see if the colleague is open and open minded enough to ask for suggestions for improvement. This is a delicate moment: how to decide if the colleague is ready for real coaching and suggestions for improvement. If the colleague folds his or her arms across his or her chest or crushes the notes savagely, the coach may presume that he or she is not open to suggestions. The coach ends the exchange by suggesting that his or her colleague observe him or her.

If the coach decides that the colleague is open to suggestions, he or she delivers suggestions in a neutral, "you" message fashion: "You might want to try. . . ." Again these suggestions for improvement are brief and not drawn out beyond the 10-minute limit for reflecting together. However this particular session concludes, the data collection notes from the observation remain in the hands of the requesting professor. The coach does not keep a copy.

What can go wrong:
- If the professor asks, "What did you think of my lesson?" instead of focusing on the request for observation, the coach could be sucked into that personalizing trap by responding with something other than "Remember you asked me to observe . . .".
- If the coach relies on memory instead of written data, written probing questions, or written suggestions for improvement, peer coaching fails at this point.

- If emotions or feelings are expressed instead of reflecting on the written data, the coach and the colleague will veer into personalization, evaluative comments, or supervisory comments.
- If the coach begins with "I feel" instead of "This data shows...", peer coaching will not occur.
- If the coach *tells* the solution instead of helping the colleague use the data to analyze the own problem, peer coaching fails.
- If the coach forces suggestions on his or her colleague before the colleague indicates a willingness to hear suggestions for improvement, peer coaching fails.
- If neither the coach nor the colleague schedules another peer coaching exchange at the end of each session, the health of this peer coaching partnership may be in doubt.

Debriefing

Did the process work for us?

The coach and colleague should ask themselves the 14 questions for debriefing listed in appendix 2. More economically, they will ask each other if peer coaching worked for them this time. They will ask who benefits most from peer coaching. If the student does not benefit from even an incremental improvement in the teaching-learning process, then everyone is wasting their time.

What can go wrong:

- If the partners omit even a brief debriefing session, the peer coaching exchange is not receiving the attention it deserves from professional educators trying to improve the act of teaching.
- If the partners cannot impersonally evaluate the peer coaching exchange, they will most probably not continue the peer coaching exchanges.

SUMMARY

In the hundreds of schools, in the five universities, and in the two national networks with which I have been personally involved in presenting, implementing, and reviewing peer coaching, teachers, leaders, and professors have been successful when they used this simple model with all of its rigid rules. Breakdowns have occurred when they have omitted some of the rules, reverted to the *telling* mode instead of the coaching mode, and imposed elements of supervision or evaluation in what is overtly a colleague-to-colleague model.

Peer coaching can succeed in making incremental improvements in the teaching-learning act. Weekly use of the pure form of peer coaching could rejuvenate teaching during the 30 weeks of a school year or the 16 weeks of a college semester enough to revolutionize and drastically improve teaching at all levels. Professors, instructors, and teachers interested enough to commit 30 minutes a week for this process of peer coaching could be the small, committed grass roots group who, in Margaret Mead's words, can change their world.

APPENDICES

APPENDIX 1

Steps in Peer Coaching:
A Detailed Guide

The requesting teacher is *T* while the coaching teacher is *C*.

STEP 1: THE TEACHER REQUESTS A
VISIT FOR PROBLEM SOLVING

A teacher requests a peer to observe a new technique of a single, specific concern in instruction or management. They set the date and time for the requested observation. Both agree on a data-gathering method such as writing down teacher questions/student responses or marking students called upon on a seating chart.

Purpose of the requested observation

T: "I'd like you to observe my (new technique to be tried, practice of a learned skill, classroom management concern)."

Lesson or activity to be observed

T: "Can you come to my class during (math, fifth period, etc.) to observe this specific concern while I teach?"

Date, time, and place for observation

C: "Which day, time, and place shall I observe you?"
C: "Do I need a seating chart?"

How shall the data be gathered?

C: "What would be the best way to record what I observe? Should I:
make tally marks on a seating chart?
use a stop watch to count seconds of wait time?
write down your questions and students' responses?
draw arrows on a seating chart to show your movements or proximity?"

Both decide on an appropriate data-gathering method.

STEP 2: THE VISIT

The coach comes to the scheduled observation with an appropriate data-gathering sheet on which he or she has already written the teacher's specific request so that he or she can focus on the singular concern. No judgment or evaluation statement is recorded. The time is recorded at the beginning, at intervals, and at the end of the observation.

Coach prepares data-gathering material beforehand.
Coach writes down the specific problem on which the teacher requested data or the new technique (such as question, pause, name) the teacher is trying.
Coach writes down beginning time.
Coach gathers data only on that specific problem or concern requested by the teacher.
Coach records data, leaving out any evaluation or judgment.
Coach marks or records time in margins, if necessary.
Coach writes down ending time.

STEP 3: REFLECTING ALONE

The coach reviews the teacher's original request for observation. The coach reviews the observation notes but does not summarize or categorize because the teacher must go through the raw data, step by step. The coach deletes any statements such as *Enough, Too much, Too little,* and so on.

On Coaching Form #1, the coach writes down

- The opening statement for step 4 (reflecting together): "Remember, you asked me to observe your . . . ?"
- Three or four neutral leading questions to keep the teacher talking and engaging in self-analysis of the lesson: "What does this data tell you?" *Never* say "How did you *feel* about your lesson?"

    Coach reviews facts and clarifies any marks because the original notes will be given to the teacher.
    Coach marks or numbers the specific facts or incidents.

- Coach may highlight categories or patterns but better not: it is better to let teacher discover patterns.

STEP 4: REFLECTING TOGETHER

The coaching teacher reviews the data gathered on the agreed-upon format, leads the requesting teacher to self-analysis, and lists some suggestions for improvement when the requesting teacher is ready.

Teacher controls this conference, asking for the factual data gathered relevant to the specific request for observation. Either the coach or the teacher restates the original request to begin the conference. The teacher looks at the data with the coach, talking through step by step. He or she analyzes the relevance of the data and begins drawing conclusions leading to solution of his or her concern. The teacher does most of the talking, asks for suggestions from the coach when he or she is ready and may ask for an additional observation and coaching session.

The coach sits beside the teacher with the notes between them. The coach walks the teacher through each step of the data collected, letting the teacher do most of the talking, and asking leading questions to help the teacher arrive at his or her own conclusions. The coach does *not* make evaluative or judgmental statements, but the teacher may make evaluative statements on his or her own. Nonverbal behavior is very important here. Equal seating with the notes shared equally is an important factor to avoid the talkative supervisory stance of an evaluator.

Teacher leads and does most of the talking.

Teacher or coach restate request for observation

T: "I asked you to observe my. . . . What facts did you record?"

Coach walks the teacher through specific facts from the notes and mentions times, if relevant.

Teacher listens to facts, talks about them, and states his or her own conclusions from the recorded data.

Teacher and coach reflect on recorded facts and their relation to the teacher's request for observation.

Coach may say:

C: "What conclusions can you reach from these data that I recorded?" "Are these enough facts to see the effects of the lesson?" "Do you want me to observe this concern in another class or on another day?"

The coach does *not* say:

C: "I *think* the lesson was excellent."

C: "How did you *feel* the lesson went?"

C: "Why did you do what you did?"

C: "You should do it this way."

C: "I have the solution to your problem."

C: "Go and observe Mr. Goodteacher: he does this correctly."

C: "You need a workshop or course in . . ."

C: "You have nothing to worry about. Those students don't pay attention in my class either."

If the teacher is ready for suggestions from the coach and indicates that receptivity, the coach pulls out the Coaching Form # 2 to talk from. Rather than handing the teacher Coaching Form # 2, he or she makes a suggestion from his or her notes and discusses it with the teacher. Other suggestions are discussed if the teacher asks for others.

STEP 5: DEBRIEFING

Process review: Did it work for us?

The teacher and coach analyze the process by asking themselves and each other a series of questions related to the method of data gathering, the talking time of both coach and teacher, and the benefits of peer coaching to the teacher, the coach, the students, and the improvement of instruction. They should plan an immediate follow-up or set an appointment to reverse the roles, maybe on the same subject or concern.

Process Review Questions for Debriefing

1. Who talked the most? Why?
2. Were there any judgments or evaluative statements made?
3. If so, how can we avoid them in the future?
4. Were feelings or recorded facts discussed?
5. Did the conference include praise or blame?
6. Was the feedback specific?

7. Did the coach's questions lead the teacher to draw conclusions?
8. Did the coach become too directive?
9. Would notes or audio recording or video recording have been better?
10. Were the facts gathered and presented in a non-evaluative manner?
11. Will the process lead to the improvement of instruction?
12. Will the teacher act as a coach?
13. Will the teacher request another observation?
14. Who—teacher or coach—benefits the most from peer coaching? (This is a trick question; the students benefit most.)

APPENDIX 2

Debriefing Questions

1. Who talked the most? Why?
2. Were there any judgments or evaluative statements made?
3. If so, how can we avoid them in the future?
4. Were feelings or recorded facts discussed?
5. Did the conference include praise or blame?
6. Was the feedback specific?
7. Did the coach's questions lead the teacher to draw conclusions?
8. Did the coach become too directive?
9. Would notes or audio recording or video recording have been better?
10. Were the facts gathered and presented in a non-evaluative manner?
11. Will the process lead to the improvement of instruction?
12. Will the teacher act as a coach?
13. Will the teacher request another observation?
14. Who—teacher or coach—benefits the most from peer coaching?

APPENDIX 3
Active Listening

POINTS FROM THOMAS GORDON'S ACTIVE LISTENING

1. Avoid ordering, directing, commanding.
2. Avoid warning, admonishing, moralizing, preaching.
3. Avoid advising, giving solutions or suggestions.
4. Avoid lecturing, teaching, giving logical examples.
5. Avoid judging, criticizing.
6. Avoid disagreeing, blaming.
7. Avoid praising, agreeing.
8. Avoid name-calling, ridiculing, shaming.
9. Avoid interpreting, analyzing, diagnosing.
10. Avoid reassuring, sympathizing, consoling, supporting.
11. Avoid probing, questioning, interrogating.
12. Avoid withdrawing, distracting, humoring, diverting (Gordon, 1977).

For further study, consult Steve Covey's Empathic Listening in *Seven Habits of Highly Effective People* (1989).

PEER COACHING: DOS AND DON'TS

Dos

1. Listen actively.
2. Pause . . . and make reflective statements.
3. Insert neutral probing questions to get the peer to continue reflection.
4. Bite your tongue . . . and let the teacher talk.
5. Let the peer fill the silent gaps.
6. Review only the written data.
7. Leave other concerns for another visit.
8. Refer to the safety of the peer coaching rules.
9. Offer to gather data using a different method.
10. Lead into another visit or exchange.

Don'ts

1. Praise.
2. Blame.
3. Judge.
4. Set yourself as an example.
5. Offer solutions on your own not supported by research or practice.
6. Talk before an adequate pause to get the other person going.
7. Offer data that is not written as observed.
8. Examine concerns that were not requested: offer no sidelines.
9. Offer to break the peer coaching rules.
10. No praise, no blame: worth repeating.

APPENDIX 4

Faculty Development: The One-Day Seminar for Peer Coaching

In the one-day seminar, the theory of peer coaching is discussed in relation to clinical supervision, formative and summative evaluation, and comparison with other models. The model of peer coaching is demonstrated with the facilitator teaching a short 10-minute lesson with the coaching problem obvious with the assistance of a co-facilitator who peer coaches using the five simple steps of the model.

After the demonstrated model is analyzed and discussed, the participants engage in guided practice so that each person acts as requesting teacher and then as peer coach. The guided practice is made simple because the facilitator teaches the short problem lesson for the guided practice with participants who are the requesting teacher in the guided practice acting as the students for the lesson. The co-facilitators give feedback to each pair during the seminar and the whole group analyzes and discusses the true coaching suggestions for improvement as the final debriefing for the present model of peer coaching.

SAMPLE AGENDA FOR PEER COACHING SEMINAR

1. Welcome and Introductions
2. Activity: Total years for each group and whole group as a professional educator.

3. Activity: Who do you coach? scout troop? choir? soccer team? child? partner? spouse?

4. Theory mini-lecture: Clinical supervision, evaluation, coaching, peer coaching, contrasting views of Popham and Hunter.

5. Joyce and Showers' Transfer of Learning Chart. If I stop now and let you read the handbook after my mini-lecture, you will retain only 5 percent of this theory and long term, use only 5 percent.

6. Demonstration: Co-facilitators demonstrate the five simple steps of peer coaching with a short mini-lesson on a non-traditional content area to capture interest of participants: Chi-san-bop, jump starting a battery with cables, taking a fish hook from an arm or potato, dance steps, or line up for a T formation in football.

7. Review Joyce and Showers' chart on Transfer of Learning. If we stop now after this demonstration, your long-term retention and use of this will be 10 percent.

8. Model the five simple steps of peer coaching and provide for guided practice: Analysis of this agenda follows Transfer of Learning Chart.

   Guided practice: participants pair up with peers, each in turn assuming the role of requesting teacher and coaching teacher.

   First practice: Co-facilitators set the problem for the pairs (e.g., the Hunter strategy of questioning with student name called after the question and a pause). Partners walk through the checklist for step 1 (requesting a visit for problem solving).

   In step 2 (the visit [simulation]), the coaching teacher gathers data on the request while the requesting teachers assume the role for this one step of acting as students to the one co-facilitator who teaches a lesson, taking the role of requesting teacher. A very brief, high interest lesson, no more than eight minutes, is taught which includes the problem of the requesting teacher.

   In step 3 (reflecting alone), the coaching teacher reviews the notes and the agreed-upon data-gathering device, reflects, and writes some suggestions for improvement if the requesting teacher seems ready to receive true peer coaching after the impartial feedback of the data-gathering device.

In step 4, pairs practice reflecting together, being careful to restate the request, show feedback, and reflect together on analyzing the lesson while being careful to show no evaluation, judgment, blame, or praise. In step 5 (debriefing), the pairs answer the process review questions and reflect aloud with the whole group.

For the second guided practice, the partners switch roles so that each can play the requesting teaching and the coaching teacher.

9. Review Joyce and Showers' chart on transfer of learning. If we stop now after this guided practice, your long-term retention and use of this technique will be 20 percent.

10. Feedback: Co-facilitators give feedback to each peer coaching pair during their two guided practices. The facilitators circulate during the guided practice and give simple feedback on the first round; then during the second round, they provide true coaching so that errors can be corrected.

11. Review Joyce and Showers' chart on transfer of learning. If we stop now after this feedback, your long-term retention and use of this will be 25 percent. If you use peer coaching in your daily practice, you will see long-term use and retention at 90 percent.

Other professions using peer coaching:
- Reach for the Stars: business peer coaching in Silicon Valley.
- "What Do You Think I Should Do?" (Brothers, 2002).

12. How will you use peer coaching to reach 90 percent transfer of learning for yourself as a professional educator and for your students?

(The complex logistics of item 8 need not be printed on the agenda. The co-facilitators need to know that one of them will teach the mini-lessons to avoid the lengthy boredom of each requesting teacher in the pair teaching a lesson, thus

increasing the time of a one-day seminar. So for the requesting teacher in each pair, he or she plays his or her own role in
steps 1, 3, 4, and 5 in the simulation for guided practice. He
or she as the requesting teacher relinquishes that role to the
facilitator during step 2 and the requesting teachers play the
roles of the facilitator's student during step 2. The coaching
teacher plays that role in all five steps.)

APPENDIX 5

Handouts for Faculty Development Seminar

Peer Coaching in Higher Education

by

Barbara Gottesman, Ed.D.
Author of
Peer Coaching for Educators
Chair (retired), Educational Leadership
College of Education
San José State University

bgott2004@sbcglobal.net
408-531-9402

MANAGING CHANGE

Adopter Types

Innovator—eager to try new ideas, open to change, willing to take risks, naïve perhaps, not always an insider.   4 percent

Leader—open to change, but more thoughtful about getting involved, trusted by other people and sought for advice and opinions.   17 percent

Early Majority—cautious and deliberate about deciding to adopt anything new, tends to be a follower, not a leader. 29 percent

Late Majority—skeptical of adopting new ideas, set in their ways, can be won over by peer pressure and administrative expectations.   29 percent

Resister—suspicious and generally opposed to new ideas, low in influence, and isolated from the main stream.   17 percent

Saboteur—from the old French sabot, wooden shoe, or to clog up the machinery by throwing in a wooden shoe to stop it.

4 percent

Modified by Shirley Hord and Barbara Gottesman for use in the South Carolina Center for School Leadership's Managing Change seminars for school teams, 1990–1995. Original work based on Gene Hall. The concerns based approach for facilitating change. *Educational Horizons* 57 (1979): 202–08.

COACHING: PEER COACHING FOR EDUCATORS

Five Steps

1. Request a visit: the teacher or person to be coached initiates the coaching process by requesting an observation of one skill or problem, involves teacher and coach.
2. Visit: observing one skill or problem, involves teacher and coach.

3. Reflecting alone: The coach reviews notes and lists some possibilities, involves only the coach.
4. Reflecting together: Talk after the visit: discussing only the actual facts and the data gathered on the skill requested to be observed, involves both teacher and coach.
5. Debriefing: Process review: analyzing the deconstruction of the observed skill and the process of coaching itself, involves both teacher and coach.

Table Appendix 5.1. Transfer of New Learning into the Daily Practice of Teaching

	Knowledge Level or Short Term (%)	Application Level or Long Term (%)
Theory	20	5
Demonstration	35	10
Modeling and Guided Practice	70	20
Feedback	80	25
Coaching	90	90

Joyce, B., & Showers, B. (1987, January). *Professional development seminar on the coaching of teaching.* Columbia: South Carolina State Department of Education.

CHECKLIST FOR THE FIVE COMPONENTS WITH MAXIMUM TIMES

1. Request for a visit (5 minutes)
   __ Observation requested
   __ Specific concern defined
   __ Coach narrows concern
   __ Confidentiality established
   __ No judgment or evaluation
   __ Lesson to be observed
   __ Data-gathering method, both decide
   __ Seating chart, if necessary
   __ Observer-coach seating or placement
   __ Time/place
   __ Time for reflecting together: talk after the visit
   Notes:

2. Visit (10 minutes)
   __ Request written at top of page as reminder
   __ Starting/ending time
   __ Method to be used to collect data
   __ Data collection on separate sheet
   __ No judgment or evaluation
   Notes:

3. Reflecting alone: Coach reviews notes and lists some possibilities
   __ Coach reviews data, deletes any evaluation, shows *only* written data collection
   __ Three leading questions listed on Coaching Form # 1
   __ No judgment or evaluation
   __ Suggestions listed on Coaching Form # 2
   Notes:

4. Reflecting together: Talk after the visit (5–10 minutes)
   __ Plan where to sit in relation to teacher
   __ Teacher or coach restatement of request in order to begin
   __ Stay away from "I" messages

___ Coach goes over *only* specific *written* data collected and makes no outside observations

___ Coach careful not to be trapped by teacher's or presenter's comments "What did you think of my lesson?"

___ Ask three leading questions to analyze data collected on the specific concern

___ Teacher analysis: get teacher talking

___ No judgment or evaluation

___ Teacher request for coaching suggestions or alternatives

___ Teacher request for further observation

___ Coach gives teacher all notes or tapes

___ Schedule another session or exchange

Notes:

5. Debriefing: Did it work for us? (3 minutes)

___ Teacher reaction to observation/coaching

___ Coach reaction to observation/coaching

___ Value of chosen data collection method

___ Conference strengths and weaknesses

___ 14 Process Review Questions

___ Who learned the most?

___ Next session?

Debriefing: Process Review Questions

1. Who talked the most? Why?
2. Were there any judgments or evaluative statements made?
3. If so, how can we avoid them in the future?
4. Were feelings or recorded facts discussed?
5. Did the conference include praise or blame?
6. Was the feedback specific?
7. Did the coach's questions lead the teacher to draw conclusions?
8. Did the coach become too directive?
9. Would notes or audio recording or video recording have been better?

10. Were the facts gathered and presented in a non-evaluative manner?
11. Will the process lead to the improvement of instruction?
12. Will the teacher act as a coach?
13. Will the teacher request another observation?
14. Who—teacher or coach—benefits the most from peer coaching?

STAGES OF CONCERN A diagnostic tool

Typical Expression of Concern (mental activity, thought, worry, analysis, anticipation, preoccupation) about an innovation

REFOCUSING – I have some ideas about something that would work even better.

COLLABORATION – I am concerned about relating what I am doing with what my co-workers are doing.

CONSEQUENCE – How is my use of the innovation affecting students? How can I refine it to have more impact?

MANAGEMENT – I seem to be spending all my time getting materials ready.

PERSONAL – How will using it affect me?

INFORMATIONAL – I would like to know more about it.

AWARENESS – I am not concerned about the innovation yet.

PEER COACHING: THREE PHASES

I. Peer watching (2 months)
   A. Four visits to another classroom
      1. Noted on record
      2. No feedback
   B. Videotapes of self
      1. Four lessons taped and watched
      2. Four tapes erased
II. Peer feedback (2 months)
   A. Training session: Five steps of peer coaching
   B. Coach offers no suggestions
   C. Four feedback sessions with peer with no suggestions, just feedback of data
III. Peer coaching (2 months)
   A. Review of five steps
   B. Coach offers suggestions when asked
   C. Four visits and four true peer coaching sessions

SPECIAL TIPS FOR STEP 4 OF PEER COACHING

Reflective Language of Collaboration

1. Paraphrase to promote reflection:
   Let me make sure I understand . . .
   What this sounds like to me is . . .
   In other words, . . .
   So . . .
2. Clarify to promote reflection:
   Tell me what you mean when you . . .
   Tell me how that idea is like (or different from) . . .
   Would you tell me a little more about . . . ?
   It would help me understand if you would give me an example of . . .
   So, are you saying or suggesting that . . . ?

3. Mediation stems: to be used only after paraphrasing and reflective items have been used.

   What do you think would happen if . . . ?

   How do you decide . . . ?

   How do you come to a conclusion about . . . ?

   What is the impact of _____ on students . . . ?

Table 2.1.   Coaching Form # 1

Request for Visit:

_____

_____

Leading Questions:

1.

_____

2.

_____

3.

_____

-----------------------------cut here and separate forms-----------------------------

Coaching Form # 2

Suggestions for changes or improvements when the teacher requests them:

1.

_____

2.

_____

3.

_____

What is another way you might . . . ?

What criteria do you use for . . . ?

4. Finding a solution together or making suggestions if the person being coached is now open to suggestions; this is to be used only after paraphrasing and reflective items and mediating items have been used.

Some teachers have tried . . .

There are several other approaches . . .

The research in this area shows that . . .

A recent article in _____said that . . .

Could we look at this topic together? I would like some more information also.

I have heard that this teacher uses _____ in her classroom.

Let's plan to visit him together.

APPENDIX 6

Examples of Actual Peer Coaching Exchanges

These examples of actual peer coaching exchanges between graduate students who are also in school and district leadership positions are offered as an example of how peer coaching can be used to solve problems in administration: colleges, universities, schools, businesses, or other groups. The exchanges are offered to illustrate the in-depth problem solving that peer coaching partners can achieve with the simple device of peer coaching.

These peer coaching exchanges illustrate problems common to both schools and colleges because they deal with race, personnel, committees, administrators versus teachers, senior faculty and junior faculty, factions, getting more money, persuading faculty to adopt new programs, and even organizational skills.

PEER COACHING CYCLE: SAMPLE # 1

Setting the scene: Latino male principal of an elementary school and an African American female principal of an elementary school from the same district but different schools. Proper names have been omitted as well as references to school and district names.

Reflections after Peer Coaching Exchanges

Peer Coaching Exchange # 1

While visiting with my peer coaching partner, I realized that this had been the first opportunity in six years as an administrator that I had formally been involved in a peer coaching cycle. As an administrator, I have had many opportunities to share my observations with teachers as we work informally on instructional best practices through our conversations and formally through the evaluation process. I have never been on the receiving end of this process.

At first it was a bit intimidating to invite a peer to look for weaknesses of mine as an administrator. The only consolation factor was that my peer seemed to be equally uncomfortable.

We talked about a variety of things about ourselves, our staff, and the challenges we saw at our schools. This gave us an idea or a reference point as we worked together with peer coaching.

Areas that I needed feedback with included effective communication tools, implementation of the Apprenticeship Approach to Literacy Learning, and lastly establishing clear expectations for my staff related to instructional practices, professional attitudes and Closing the Achievement Gap (CTAG) practices which were courageous conversation. We set our first meeting for Tuesday, September 25. My peer coaching partner would observe a steering committee meeting with my grade level representatives. She would be looking for indicators demonstrating preparation, concise delivery of information, and pacing that allowed us to start and end on time. My steering committee meeting would begin promptly at 7:30 a.m. and would be scheduled to end at 8:00 a.m.

Peer Coaching Exchange # 2

My peer coaching partner arrived at my steering committee meeting and quietly observed as I conducted the meeting. I could not help but look over every time I saw her jotting down notes on her note pad. I continued with my meeting. I first went through the agenda items that were informational in nature and concluded with giving teachers an opportunity to talk about grade level points for discussion, questions, and concerns. As my agenda items took longer than anticipated due to the questions generated, we were not able to finish agenda items brought forth by the steering committee members.

After the meeting, my peer coaching partner asked me the following reflective questions for peer coaching:

1. Is there a reason why there is not time allocated to each agenda item?
2. When can agenda items from teachers be placed on the agenda?
3. Can you think of another structure that would allow teachers to have equal air time?
4. What would be the benefit for yourself and for the teachers?

After having some time for reflection as well as some consultation time with my district mentor, I made some changes. First of all, we began our meeting by having teachers' agenda items first. We allocated the first 15 minutes for teachers' items and the second 15 minutes for my items as principal. This allowed me to bring importance and status to teacher agenda items as well as added flexibility if we need to go longer on teacher items without cutting them off.

It was also noted that it would have been a powerful model for teachers to see the principal involved in a peer coaching cycle. I never acknowledged the purpose of my partner's visit other than to say she was visiting. As peer coaching is an important part of the apprenticeship model teachers are implementing at our school, this would have been a great opportunity. There will be other opportunities.

Peer Coaching Exchange # 3

Early in the school year, it was announced that two of our veteran teachers would be retiring. These two teachers are upper grade teachers at the same grade level. As I was trying to move forward with the concept of the Apprenticeship Approach to Literacy Learning (AALL), I was confronted by statements such as "Well, I don't think I will do this. . . . It is my last year. . . . I just want to enjoy my last year." I needed to find a way to change the attitudes of these two teachers. Both teachers were very well liked, and like it or not, were models to our new teachers. In order for AALL to be successful, all had to buy in. I had several conversations with my peer coach and my district mentor about an approach that would change the perspective of these two retiring teachers.

A couple of ideas came out. The first was to spotlight the accomplishments of the careers of these two teachers by acknowledging some genuine instructional accomplishments publicly and through what would become the Exemplary Staff section of the Monday Memo. It was also a strategy to have our in-house professional development trainers (two master teachers) to seek out actively their input and whenever possible assign competence to them in Teacher Expectations Student Achievement (TESA). Lastly I personally met with both teachers and acknowledged the significance of their accomplishments as well as their powerful influence over our new teachers. It would be my request for them to participate actively during our professional development opportunities to the fullest extent possible. Their legacy of stellar professional development in the year of their retirement would be impressive. Every other upper grade teacher was a new teacher except one: the veterans could have enormous influence. As veteran teachers, they relied on their years of experience to know what to do. New teachers rely greatly on who they see as their mentors and role models. The two retiring teachers agreed to participate in the new staff development program and not to engage in conversations that would suggest that AALL was a waste of time.

Peer Coaching Exchange # 4

My peer coach was scheduled to observe my staff meeting, but she was unable to make it at the last minute. I asked my district mentor to observe and make some comments since he and I met on a regular basis anyway. Some interesting points came out. My district mentor noted that I tended to over-explain things during staff meetings. In a smaller group or one-on-one, I am very concise and clear with the message I am trying to deliver. However, when I am in front of my staff as a whole group, I over-explain items which seemed to cause some frustration among teachers. After reflecting upon and analyzing this point, I had further discussion with my district mentor. I realized that I did this as a defense mechanism. I was afraid of follow up questions from teachers so I tried to cover as many scenarios as possible in my explanation in order not to be attacked by teachers. This was just paranoia. From that point on, my mentor had a sign for me when he noticed that I was over-explaining.

Peer Coaching Exchange # 5

Since the beginning of the school year, the Administrators of Color group in our district has been struggling with a very serious concern. My partner, as the chairperson of our group, approached me as her peer coach for guidance and support. One of our fellow administrators was having a difficult time with the culture of the district as well as the everyday dealings of being an African American principal in our school district. Through many conversations within our group of six, we established a social support system to our new colleague as well as a professional support system for him. In essence, we were collaboratively trying to establish a complex coaching process for him. We were all concerned about his ability to succeed in the district.

It was becoming very evident to me how powerful peer coaching had been for me and the subsequent changes I have made because of feedback and reflection. It was also made very evident that peer coaching would only work if there is a willingness to hear feedback and to be coached.

We ended up planning an entire retreat to work on building trust which would allow us to coach our African American colleague. What we hoped to be a productive time to connect with each other, build trust, and bring support to our colleague ended up as something quite different. As my peer coach and I planned this whole day retreat, we planned a coaching scenario that would allow our colleague to see guiding questions and how they could be used to bring about reflective thinking which could assist with decision making.

Peer Coaching Exchange # 6

I went to my peer coach's school for a school site council meeting which my partner was conducting. One of the council members is a challenge, and thus my peer coaching partner feels that at times she is short with her in front of the group. I would be looking for changes in body language, tone, and visual contact when my partner addressed this council member. Her goal, of course, is to get through the meeting without having to worry about the reason for my being there.

The meeting started well. My partner went through several agenda items until this challenging council member asked her a question. As an item of information, the principal and several teachers were planning to attend a diversity conference at Newport Beach. The challenging council member (CCm) could not believe it was necessary for the principal and her staff to continue to get more training in this area. The CCm was interested in how the trip would be funded and why it was necessary to attend when they had already had extensive training in CTAG. The CCm noted that the entire staff had already been involved in the Beyond Diversity Conference and did not see a need for this trip. The CCm's demeanor was not particularly aggressive or disrespectful, but you could tell she felt strongly about this expenditure.

The principal, my peer coaching partner, paused for a few seconds before responding. She leaned forward slightly, clasped her hands, and spoke in a voice a bit lower than her usual tone. This may have had a calming effect, but her eye contact relayed a different message. As she moved forward, her head moved lightly down. As she looked at the CCm, it reminded me of someone who has just looked up from reading the paper with bifocals on. After a bit, the principal realized the effect her look had on the CCm and changed both her tone, her body position (leaned back a bit), and looked around at other members of the council as she talked about the necessity for this trip.

After the meeting, I asked the principal how she felt when the CCm asked about the trip. She admitted that she was a bit steamed since she had already informed the group about this conference and that the CCm had no objections when she brought it up previously. I asked her to recall her body language as she began speaking to the CCm. She did realize what she was doing and readjusted herself to a less intimidating position. She was glad I was there since it made her realize that her suspicions about herself were correct. During my visit, my presence was a reminder to her of the problem; and she was able to monitor and adjust her body language.

Peer Coaching Exchange # 7

I got a call from my peer coaching partner today. Yesterday she had an experience she could not get out of her mind. We were at a meeting with a group of principals who would be affected by the budget cuts in the district. At this meeting, we began talking about how money from voluntary integration program (VIP) funds would be allocated. It was the task of this committee, which included seven principals, to reduce the VIP budget by $40,000 to $80,000. On the chopping block was the pre-Kindergarten program at two of the schools.

As part of the discussion, my peer coaching partner and another principal greatly affected by this proposal expressed points of view that were uncomfortable. My partner felt badly about this exchange since all she was doing during this process was to identify a need for funding for her school. Her intention was not to take anything from anyone. However, this was not how her comments were interpreted.

Of course, both my partner and the other principal left the meeting feeling very much in conflict. I actually had an opportunity to talk with both principals about this situation. The advice to both was the same: talk to each other and work out this misunderstanding.

Comments were made by each that could be interpreted as hurtful but were not intended to be so. The only way to get past this situation was for them to meet and to clarify what was meant by the comments each made during the meeting. They agreed to contact each other. As I spoke with my partner who had called me, I did not mention that I had spoken with both of them about this situation. I wonder if I should have.

Reflection in Action

Which partner gained most from the peer coaching exchanges?
How did the peer coaching partnership influence other interactions?

PEER COACHING CYCLE: SAMPLE # 2

The second illustrative peer coaching cycle follows more traditional examples of physically observing and giving feedback on site.

Setting the scene: assistant principal elementary school, white female; assistant principal, two elementary schools, white male, from the same district but different schools. Proper names have been omitted as well as references to school and district names.

Reflective Journal Entries after a Peer Coaching Exchange

November 7

I asked my peer coach to observe me as I conducted a post-observation evaluative conference with a third grade teacher. The teacher has returned to teaching; it is her second year in this school; and it is her first year in third grade with a class size of 20. I wanted my peer coach to watch my style and see if I was directive enough with the teacher while continuing our trusting relationship. I was pleased at the end of the teacher conference when my peer coach and I debriefed. He had picked up on the two main points I wanted to get across to the teacher: improvement of her questioning techniques and narrowing her focus during the lesson. My peer coach gave me feedback that I have been directive with the teacher but in a collegial sense. I offered her some written information on questioning techniques and tried to lead her to pick out areas for improvement. Although I reflected that I did most of the talking, my peer coach said that I was asking probing question to lead the teacher to the correct conclusions. This was helpful to me, and I look forward to watching my partner during his own post-observation conference next week.

November 12

I observed my peer coaching partner as he conducted a post-observation conference with a third grade teacher at his site. The teacher has six years of experience, and my partner had a very good rapport with her. I was especially impressed with my partner's body language and eye contact. The teacher knew he was genuinely interested in what she had to say, and my partner practiced active listening very well. In fact, the teacher asked his advice about one thing that happened during the lesson. When a struggling student had answered a difficult question, the students in the classroom spontaneously applauded. The teacher wanted to know if this was OK or was it saying to the student that he usually doesn't know the answer but hooray because he finally did? My partner used an analogy from his own teaching experience and assured the teacher that this was a good sign that the students were working as a team and were proud of this student. My partner tactfully brought up the suggestion that the teacher seemed to be teaching to one side of the classroom. She was unaware of this and thanked my partner for the heads up. I think the teacher and my partner talked an equal amount of time. My partner asked her very good questions to lead her to draw her own conclusions.

November 14

During the class break, I asked my peer coaching partner about a process he had mentioned during the conference with the teacher the other day. It is a self-esteem idea for students. On a voluntary basis, teachers are assigned two students who are not in their classrooms. These students have low self-esteem, could be behavior problems, or are extremely shy. The teacher makes it a point to introduce himself or herself to the student and then continues to make contact with that student twice a week for the rest of the school year. The contact is brief and casual to find out how the day is going for the student. My partner says this idea has had amazing results for some children just to know that there is an adult on campus who truly cares for the student. The relationships that are formed usually last for years until the student leaves the school. This seems like such a simple solution, and I definitely want to try it when I am a site principal.

December 4

My peer coaching partner e-mailed me with some questions about organization. He wanted to know how my office looks so clean and organized: Did I make an effort to make sure all things are filed as fast as possible? Did I get help from the secretaries? What are my organizational techniques? Did my office always look like this or was it a mess at one time?

I responded to my partner's questions by giving him some of the organization techniques I use: filing the papers on my desk at least once a week, getting rid of papers that were outdated or if it was a task I have completed; and having a folder for each month so that I file papers in that file which need to be saved or have a deadline during that month. I also gave him the titles I use for my files to keep everything organized. I think it is difficult for my partner because he is assistant principal at two schools and never has time at either one to just do organization.

December 9

My peer coaching partner and I spoke about how I organize my English Language Learners Advisory Committee (ELLAC) at my school.

He told me that at his school, the parents voted to be represented by the school site council (SSC). My reply was that at my school our problem was that we had no second language parents on the SSC so the council made decisions about our English language learners but didn't know anything about them. The ELLAC has been an impetus for making our second language parents feel welcome at the school, and they are getting brave enough to voice their opinions if they have a concern. If the PTA board and the SSC are all Caucasian like my school, then there really is not any representation for parents of students of other ethnicities or languages. ELLAC parents are now volunteering at school and participating in other activities because the school is more inclusive now.

December 9

The other part of our session was my question to my partner about his role in the district safety program. He spent eight years as assistant principal and district safety officer. I wanted to know what administrative and managerial strategies he gained from that experience. He told me about the difficulty of putting together a program that was new to the district and to the area. He became familiar with city officials and representatives from the police and fire departments. It has given him insight on how to make a school safe from disaster and ideas on how to make a successful program work, starting from the vision all the way from implementation. He learned many new communications skills from this process which he shared with me.

Reflection in Action

How did the direct observations as a basis for peer coaching differ from the casual conversations or asking advice?
Which seem to benefit the partners more?

APPENDIX 7
Participatory Decision Making

Participatory decision making is a decision-making process which ensures the full participation of all stakeholders and illustrates the use of democratic, inclusive, and collaborative processes by leaders, educators, teachers, professors, and students in a learning community. It was designed by Dr. Barbara Gottesman and has been extensively used with widely varying small groups.

Definition: a collaborative effort involving opportunity for equal input and equal participation by all members of the team.

Purpose: to list solutions, possibilities, or actions for the team to implement.

Outcomes: an equal chance for input in a structured setting is the same as an equal responsibility for action.

Roles: to be rotated at each team meeting:
Time keeper
Recorder
Task master
Name caller
Materials supplier
Host

Counter

Process observer

(Some roles may be omitted or one person may serve two roles, depending on the number in the group.)

Materials: Call bells

Pens or magic markers

Paper

Chart paper

Post-It notes

One pencil

Masking tape

Ideas

Setting: Adult tables

Adult chairs

Five to seven persons in each group

PARTICIPATORY DECISION MAKING

1. Define the task. (Task master makes this statement.)
2.. Set time limits. (Time keeper makes this statement. For a trial run, try 3 minutes for step # 3, 10 minutes for step # 4 [includes 5 and 6], 3 minutes for step # 7, 8 minutes for step # 8, 5 minutes for step # 9, and repeating it.)
3. Silent generation: Each team member silently generates ideas and lists them briefly on his or her own paper or one idea each on a Post-It note.
4. Structured sharing: Name caller calls on each team member in turn, going clockwise. As his or her name is called, each team member reads one idea from his or her written list or from his or her Post-It notes. No discussion, no explanation, no defense, and no clarification. If the idea has already been contributed, the team member reads another of his or her listed ideas. When the team member runs out of listed ideas, he or she says "Pass." (At any time, one idea may stimulate another idea, so

team members may add ideas to their own lists during the structured sharing.)

Task master: If a team member begins to elaborate on his or her idea (or explain or discuss or defend or clarify), the task master must ding him or her. If any one interrupts another team member at any time, the task master dings him or her. If the alert task master hears side conversations, it is his or her duty to ding the side conversations.

5. During the structured sharing, the recorder records contributed ideas on paper or chart paper or places the Post-It notes, one idea at a time on a wall.

6. The name caller keeps calling the names of team members around the circle until all team member say pass or he or she can see that all ideas are exhausted . . . or until the time limits are reached.

7. Clarification only: With the recorder leading the discussion, the team members look at the master list and may ask or give clarification only. No elaboration or in-depth explanations are allowed at this point . . . and certainly no value judgments. Post-It notes may be rearranged in categories, but none shall be eliminated at this point.

8. Relative merits discussion: The teams discuss the relative merits of the ideas within the time limits.

9. Weighted value: The weighted-value process is thoughtful and efficient. As the recorder reads aloud each idea listed on the master list, each team member raises one, two, or three fingers, depending on the weighted value he or she wishes to assign to it. (Three fingers showing is the heaviest weighted value.) The recorder counts (and asks an assistant counter to check his or her figures) and adds the total for each idea and writes it on the chart in pencil. This should be done silently.

10. Time lapse or break: 5 or 10 minutes, overnight, or next meeting. Repeat process with first set of sums covered or erased.

11. Arrive at consensus.

Critical Attributes

1. Roles are breakdowns of the components of the traditional leader role. No one can dominate. The focus is on the team effort.

2. Requiring team members to write silently in step 3 puts the brain in gear before it puts the mouth in motion.

3. Call bells are a fun but firm strategy for eliminating the side conversations, the personal interruptions, and lengthy explanations. The "dinging" also ensures that no one person dominates.

4. Setting time limits for at least one step in the process helps team members focus on time management and avoid wasting time on "not essential to this process" baggage.

5. Requiring team members to say "Pass" during step 4 is a key element. This rule reinforces the idea that every team member has an equal opportunity for input.

6. Separating the components of the decision-making process "Silent Generation," "Structured Sharing," and "Clarification Only" from "Relative Merits Discussion" and the silent "Weighted-Value" helps team members focus on the critical attributes instead of getting distracted by other baggage or side issues.

7. Repeating the "weighted-value" step with a break of minutes, hours, days, or weeks gives team members time to reflect on the weighted value of each idea or to discuss it with others if they wish or need to if they act as a representative on the team for a client group.

8. This is not true consensus where the team could wait minutes, hours, days, weeks, months, or years for the team to reach almost spiritual consensus, but it is as close to consensus as we are likely to get.

9. Consensus avoids a vote. In a vote, one side wins, the other loses. In this team process, we want the decision-making team to become a true action team.

10. Since this is a program designed by Barbara Gottesman, you may copy this document for school purposes as long as the copyright symbol and name are printed on each page.

APPENDIX 8

Contrast between Purposes of Coaching and Evaluating by a Supervisor

Table Appendix 8.1. Contrast between Purposes of Coaching and Evaluating by a Supervisor

Coaching		Evaluating
Enhance student success		Certify instructional effectiveness
Improve teaching-learning environment		Enforce contractual requirements
Resolve problems hindering learning		Guarantee minimum uniformity
Clear up student behavior problems		Meet legal requirements
Increase instructional diversity		Monitor professional conduct
Align student characteristics, curriculum, instruction, and evaluation		Apply district criteria for teacher effectiveness
Deepen teacher's sense of efficacy		Recognize and reward superior performance
Protect students from incompetent teachers		Protect teachers from unprofessional administrators
		Validate the district personnel selection process
	Methods	
Build trust between teachers		Judge teacher effectiveness
Engage teacher in thinking about teaching		Rate teacher (1) to continue in the same assignment, (2) transfer, (3) promote, (4) needing to improve, or (5) dismiss
Promote teacher decision making		
Promote teacher autonomy		
Peer/colleague	**Relationship**	Administrator/superior
Teachers	**Sources of Criteria**	Education code, board policy, and administrative regulation
Formative and cyclical	**Timing**	Summative and terminal
Given to requesting teacher	**Placement of Data Collected**	In personnel file
By requesting teacher	**Value Judgments**	By administrator
Determined by teacher	**Observer's Role**	Determined by administrator

Adapted from Popham, W. J. (1988). The dysfunctional marriage of formative and summative teacher evaluation. *Journal of Personnel Evaluation, 1*, 269–73, and Hunter, M. (1993). Enhancement of teaching through coaching, supervision, and evaluation. *Evaluation Perspectives, 3*(1), 1–2, 7.

BIBLIOGRAPHY

Author. (1996). Interstate School Licensure Consortium Standards for School Leaders. (ISSLC). www.ccsso.org.

Barth, R. (1990). *Improving schools from within: Teachers, parents, and principals can make a difference*. San Francisco: Jossey-Bass.

Berry, B. (1988, April). Adapting PAL activities for administrative preparation and inservice training programs. New Orleans: Paper presented at the annual conference of the American Educational Research Association.

Berry, B. (1990). Overcoming obstacles to peer coaching for principals. *Educational Leadership*, 47 (8), 62–64.

Blanchard, K. (2001). *Leadership behavior analysis II: Self assessment and scoring*. Escondido, CA: Ken Blanchard Companies.

Brothers, J. (2002). 'What do you think I should do?' *Parade Magazine*. September 1, 8–9.

Caine, R., & Caine, G. (1991). *Making connections: Teaching and the human brain*. Alexandria, VA: ASCD.

Calabrese, R. (2002). *The leadership assignment: Creating change*. Boston: Allyn and Bacon.

Cogan, M. (1961). *Supervision at the Harvard-Newton summer school*. Unpublished manuscript. Cambridge: Harvard Graduate School of Education.

Cogan, M. (1973). *Clinical supervision*. Boston: Houghton Mifflin Co.

Costa, A., & Garmston, R. (1994). *Cognitive coaching: A foundation for renaissance schools*. Norwood, MA: Christopher-Gordon Pub.

Costa, A., & Kallick, B. (1993). Through the lens of a critical friend. *Educational Leadership*, 51 (2), 49–51.

Covey, S. (1989). *Seven habits of highly effective people*. New York: Free Press.

Covey, S. (1991). *Principle-centered leadership*. New York: Summit Books.

Draughon, B., & Hord, S. (1986). Even champions have coaches: Principals provide professional development for their peers. *The Journal of Staff Development*, 7 (2), 81–90.

Educational Leadership. (1987). Collegial learning. 45 (3).

Educational Leadership. (1987). Staff development through coaching. 44 (5).

Educational Leadership. (1989). Refining supervision. 46 (8).

Educational Leadership. (1993, October). New roles, new relationships. 51 (2).

Elliott, D., & Harris, R. (1998). *Coaching teachers for education reform*. 3rd edition. Claremont, CA: Learning Light.

Fink, E., & Resnick, L. (2001). Developing principals as instructional leaders. *Phi Delta Kappan*, 82 (8), 598–606.

Garmston, R. (1988). A call for collegial coaching. *The Developer* (National Staff Development Council) 1, 4–6.

Garmston, R. (2003). Group wise. *Journal of Staff Development*, 24 (1), 1–5.

Garmston, R., with Linder, C., & Whitaker, J. (1993). Reflections on cognitive coaching. *Educational Leadership*, 51 (2), 57–61.

Gibble, J., & Lawrence, J. (1987). Peer coaching for principals. *Educational Leadership*, 45 (3), 72–73.

Gladwell, M. (2000). *The tipping point: How little things make a big difference*. Broadview Heights, OH: Wheeler Publishing.

Gladwell, M. (2005). *Blink: The power of thinking without thinking*. New York: Allen Lane.

Gladwell, M. (2008). *Outliers: The story of success*. New York: Little, Brown and Company.

Glatthorn, A. (1987). Cooperative professional development: Peer-centered options for teacher growth. *Educational Leadership*, 45 (3), 31–35.

Glatthorn, A. (1984). *Differentiated supervision*. Alexandria, VA: ASCD.

Glickman, C. (1995). *Supervision of instruction: A developmental approach*. Boston: Allyn and Bacon.

Goldhammer, R. (1969). *Clinical supervision: Special methods for the supervision of teachers*. New York: Holt, Rinehart, and Winston

Goldhammer, R., Anderson, R., & Krajewski, R. (1980). *Clinical supervision: Special methods for the supervision of teachers*. 2nd edition. New York: Holt, Rinehart & Winston.

Gordon, T. (1977). *Leader effectiveness training.* New York: Putnam.

Gottesman, B. (2000). *Peer coaching for educators.* 2nd edition. Lanham, MD: Scarecrow University Press.

Gottesman, B., & Jennings, J. (1994). *Peer coaching for educators.* Lancaster, PA: Technomic Publishers.

Guiney, E. (2001). Coaching isn't just for athletes: The role of teacher leaders. *Phi Delta Kappan,* 82 (10), 740–43.

Hall, C. (2001, February 5). Finding a niche improving the "Smart Buts." *San Jose Mercury News,* PC 1.

Hall, G., & Hord, S. (2001). *Implementing change: Patterns, Principles, and Potholes.* Boston: Allyn and Bacon.

Hord, S. (1987). *Taking charge of change.* Alexandria, VA: ASCD.

Hargreaves, A., & Dawe, R. (1989, March). Coaching as unreflective practice: Contrived collegiality or collaborative culture? Paper presented at AERA annual conference in San Francisco.

Haskins, D. (2001). *Parent as coach: Helping your teen build a life of confidence, courage and compassion.* Portland: White Oaks Resources, Inc.

Hessel, K., & Holloway, J. (2002). *A framework for school leaders: Linking the ISLLC standards to practice.* Princeton, NJ: ETS.

Hunter, M. (1971). *Teaching for transfer.* El Segundo, CA: ITIP Publications.

Hunter, M. (1979) *Mastery teaching.* El Segundo, CA: ITIP Publications.

Hunter, M. (1993). Enhancement of teaching through coaching, supervision, and evaluation. *Evaluation Perspectives,* 3 (1), 1–2, 7.

Huntley, H. (2000, April). Reach for the stars with coaching. *San Jose Mercury News,* PC 1.

Johnson, S., & Birkeland, S. (2003). The schools that teachers choose. *Educational Leadership,* 60 (8), 20–24.

Joyce, B., & Showers, B. (1982). The coaching of teaching. *Educational Leadership,* 40 (1), 4–10.

Joyce, B., Showers, B., & Rolheiser-Bennet, C. (1987). Staff development and student learning: A synthesis of research on models of teaching. *Educational Leadership,* 45 (2), 11–23.

Joyce, B., & Showers, B. (1987, January). *Professional development seminar on the coaching of teaching.* Columbia: South Carolina State Department of Education..

Levine, S. (1987). Peer support for women in management. *Educational Leadership,* 45 (3), 374–75.

Marzono, R. (2003). *What works in schools: Translating research into action.* Alexandria, VA: ASCD.

McCarthy, B. (1993). *Hemispheric mode indicator.* Wauconda, IL: About Learning.

McCarthy, B. (1999). *Leadership behavior inventory.* Wauconda, IL: About Learning, Inc.

McCarthy, B. (2000). *Learning type measure Form N.* Wauconda, IL: About Learning, Inc.

Minsky, M. (1985). *The society of the mind.* New York: Simon and Schuster.

Mosher, R., & Purpel, D. (1972). *Supervision: The reluctant profession.* Boston: Houghton-Mifflin Company.

Murphy, C. (1985). Coaching teachers. *Research Action Brief.* Washington, DC: National Institute of Education. 26 (1), 4–5.

Munro, P., & Elliott, J. (1987). Instructional growth through peer coaching. *Journal of Staff Development,* 8 (1), 25–28.

Nolan, J., & Francis, P. (1992). Changing perspectives in supervision. In Glickman, C. (editor). *Supervision in transition.* Alexandria, VA: ASCD Yearbook.

Nolan, J., & Hillkirk, K. (1991). The effects of a reflective coaching project for veteran teachers. *Journal of Curriculum and Supervision,* 7 (1), 62–76.

Noddings, N. (2003). *Caring: A feminine approach to ethics and moral education.* 2nd edition. Berkeley: University of California Press.

Nolan, J., Hawks, B., & Francis, P. (1993). Case studies: Windows onto clinical supervision. *Educational Leadership,* 51(2), 52–56.

Office of Educational Research and Improvement (OERI). *Leadership in Educational Administration Development (LEAD) Program.* Washington, DC: OERI, 1986.

Olsen, L. (1992, May). 'Critical friends' in Re: Learning faculty help colleagues navigate school reform. *Education Week,* 1, 15.

Poole, W. (1994). Removing the "super" from supervision. *Journal of Curriculum and Supervision,* 9 (3), 284–309.

Porter, D. (1992). *Strength deployment inventory.* Pacific Palisades, CA: Personal Strengths, Inc.

Popham, W. J. (1988). The dysfunctional marriage of formative and summative teacher evaluation. *Journal of Personnel Evaluation,* 1, 269–73.

Pryor, F. (1994). Ask questions even when you know the answers. *Coaching skills for managers and supervisors.* Fred Pryor Career Track Seminars.

Restak, R. (1984). *The brain.* New York: Bantam Books.

Robbins, P. (1991). *How to plan and implement a peer coaching program.* Alexandria, VA: ASCD.

Rogers, S. (1987). If I can see myself, I can change. *Educational Leadership*, 45 (2), 64–67.

Rooney, J. (1993). Teacher evaluation: No more "super" vision. *Educational Leadership*, 51 (2), 43–44.

Sarason, S. (1991). *The predictable failure of educational reform: Can we change course before it's too late?* San Francisco: Jossey Bass.

Sergiovanni, T. (1987). *The principalship—A reflective practice perspective.* Boston: Allyn and Bacon, Inc.

Showers, B. (1985). Teachers coaching teachers. *Educational Leadership*, 42 (7), 43–48.

Showers, B. (1984, October). *Peer coaching: A strategy for facilitating transfer of training.* Eugene, OR: Center for Educational Policy and Management.

Showers, B., & Joyce, B. (1996). The evolution of peer coaching. *Educational Leadership*, 53(6), 12–16.

Sizer, H. (1992). *Horace's school: Redesigning the American high school.* New York: Houghton Mifflin.

Snyder, K. (1979). *Instructional improvement: A systems approach.* Prepared for Greensboro, NC Public Schools. Lubbock, TX: Pedamorphosis, Inc.

Snyder, K. (1993). School transformation: The context for professional coaching and problem solving. In Anderson, R., & Snyder, K. (editors). *Clinical supervision and coaching for higher performance.* Lancaster, PA: Technomic Publishers.

Speck, M., & Krovetz, M. (1996). Developing effective peer coaching experiences for school administrators. *ERS Spectrum*, 14 (1), 37–42.

Sternberg, R., Ed. (1985). *Human abilities: An information-processing approach.* New York: W. H. Freeman and Company.

Sullivan, C. (1980). *Clinical supervision: A state of the art review.* Alexandria, VA: ASCD.

Sylwester, R. (1995). *A celebration of neurons: An educator's guide to the human brain.* Alexandria, VA: ASCD.

Truesdale, B., & Williams, B. (2003, October). Get off the bench and into the game with peer coaching. Peoria, IL: I. P. A. Principals Professional Conference.

Walen, E., & De Rose, M. (1993). The power of peer appraisals. *Educational Leadership*, 51 (2), 45–48.

Wolfe, P. (2001). *Brain matters: Translating research into classroom practice.* Alexandria, VA: ASCD.

Yim, Su-Jin. (2001). Ready, set . . . goal. *The Oregonian*, April 11, 2001, 2–3.